Dedication

To my husband Chris, my fellow cat lover. We lost each other and then found each other again seventeen years later. How lucky for me!

Table of Contents

Chapter One

Our Decrepit Mothers

"You're fat!" my ninety-two year old mother loudly informs my husband Chris one morning.

"Yes Mum, I know I'm fat. Now do you need me to do anything else for you before I go to work?"

My husband is a saint. Every morning he spends the first three hours of his day doing crosswords with her and taking care of everything that needs doing in the household because I am already at work. He feeds cat, brings the newspapers and mail in, takes out the garbage and recycling and serves her tea and breakfast.

"Just a little bit more milk, if you please."

"Ok Mum, and then I'm off. See you later," he dutifully replies.

She will only be alone for a few hours because he works the afternoon shift and I will get home from my teaching job just down the street soon after the three o'clock bell.

Now he is on his way to work as a city bus driver, but he will stop in at his own mother's house on the way and complete five other little jobs for her. She lives near us and is virtually bed-ridden after beating cancer. Her husband died two years ago so she lives with Chris' schizophrenic brother, Terry, who is able to help with some daily routines, but not others.

"Hi Mom, how are you feeling? I only have ten minutes so what are the top priorities that need doing this morning?"

She can see that he's in uniform and already knows the drill, so she has a list beside the bed.

"Honey, could you please bring me the leftover fruit salad from the fridge and the newspaper and change the dog's water? There's a bottle of blue pills on the kitchen table that I need, and please grab the kitchen garbage on the way out. Thank you, Dear."

"Okay Mom. Is Terry taking his medication?"

"Yes, I'm reminding him now that you showed me how to schedule an alarm on my phone."

"Okay I love you, and I'll see you tomorrow."

He is finally off to work, which will be a nice eight-hour reprieve from mother care.

Meanwhile, I am helping autistic children finish their schoolwork so they can take a break in the sensory room. Now we have finished math and are jumping on two mini-trampolines while throwing sponges to knock down the standing stuffed doll targets lined up along a bookshelf. The timer is set for five minutes, after which we will be playing Lego for five and then walking on the balance beam and then back to class.

I get a text from the secretary that my mother would like me to call. The boys are happy and busy, so I do this right away.

"Hi Mum. What's up?"

"The tree man called, and he wants to come this Saturday to prune the back garden. Is that okay with you?"

"Sure Mum, but you don't need to call me at work for that. You can just make the decision or wait until I get home. I'm not really supposed to take personal calls unless it's an emergency, like if you've fallen down and broken your hip or something."

She reluctantly agrees to respect my boundaries with some muttering under her breath and hangs up. Chris texts me that his bus broke down, so he's waiting for a mechanic and playing Tetris on his phone. Meanwhile, the boys are complaining that the timer is beeping, and I haven't got the Lego box down from the top shelf yet. I can't wait for lunch hour at this point. Just shoot me.

After school, I go home to find that Mum has pulled all her old files out of her desk one by one to reorganize, however she cannot lift them back in because she is worn out, and they are now spread out all over the floor.

"I am too tired to deal with this now, Mum. Let's take a break and have a cup of tea."

If you are English, then you already know that a cup of tea is the answer to everything. Even if somebody dies, a cup of tea will fix it.

I start cutting up veggies for dinner, and this is one job Mum can still manage and feel like she's making a useful contribution so I move the cutting board and compost bin beside her while I prep the meat and rice. I desperately want to distract her from the pile of papers in the next room, so this is a good interim solution.

After supper, I would love to watch *Entertainment Tonight*, but she can't stand anything to do with popular culture, so we are watching a *Masterpiece Mystery* until Chris gets home from work. Then she will ride the electric stair-chair downstairs to watch her own programs. She respects the television needs of the man of the house, but not mine. I heat up his supper in the microwave while he gets changed into pajama pants and a T-shirt. Then we get a couple of hours of sanity together before it starts all over again on repeat.

He tells me he's worried about his forty-four-year-old brother not taking his meds. Terry has been known to hide them before and is showing signs again. He has been talking to himself more and has forgotten to walk the dog twice this week. Despite his mother reminding him, he may still choose to ignore her. It's very difficult to enforce unless she watches him take his cocktail of pills, but this makes him angry. It was easier when he lived in the group home.

As Mum rides up on the stair-chair, we usually loudly sing the 1960's TV theme song, "Rollin', rollin', rollin' Rawhide," which makes her giggle like a little girl. Then we always turn off the TV and chat with her for fifteen minutes while she has her usual bedtime snack of half a cup of milk and two crackers with hummus. This has all been laid out during the commercials, of course. Chris tells her bus stories about his day and tries to make her laugh. The cat appears and likes to be part of the conversation. His name is Orange, and he is a shaggy beast, weighing in at twenty-six pounds. He once fought off a raccoon and then went to the vet to have his wounds stitched up. He is ornery as hell, and when we moved in, both our cats ran away within forty-eight hours to get away from him, but Mum adores him.

I make our work sandwiches and pack the lunches into the fridge. Then we bid her good-night and watch one more show just to make sure she gets into bed successfully without any mishaps.

At three o'clock in the morning we are jolted awake from our deepest sleep as the Homecare alarm screeches. Our hearts are racing in panic. A man's voice yells through the loudspeaker, "Joan this is Homecare. Are you okay? Please respond."

"She's fine, she just rolled over and hit her alarm bracelet by accident!" I yell into the telephone box.

Mum apologizes profusely for waking us up. After much swearing, we fall back asleep.

It's finally Saturday, the blessed weekend has arrived at last. Now we commence the blur of activity that will see us through the week. Go to the gym for our only weekly workout, groceries, liquor store, gift for whoever has a birthday coming up, kitty litter, drugstore, recycling sorted. Sunday is reserved for doing as little as possible, mostly drinking coffee, watching football and napping. However, Mum will often badger me into tending her huge garden that is falling into desperate disarray.

"Can you please prune the lilac bush today?"

I groan and reluctantly agree to give her an hour. She wheels her walker across the grass to bark orders at me while I do all the work.

"Not those secateurs, they are too dull. Use the loppers for the bigger branches. No, go lower on the branch to where the first shoots are growing. Take off everything higher than your shoulders. Now wrap the wire mesh around it. Push the stakes back into the ground to secure it. Roll the green bin around to collect all the branches. Go kill yourself."

After she totters back into the house, I shove the surplus branches under the back bushes to avoid making three more trips to fill up the neighbour's bins with our overflow. She will never know. I curse the fifteen other jobs I will never get away with ignoring out here. Every Sunday the nagging will resume until the end of time or until the snow falls, god willing.

Meanwhile, things are deteriorating over at Chris' mother's house. Her kidney function keeps getting worse at every check-up and it looks like she is heading for dialysis. One day we get a call that she is too weak to get out of bed, so we call an ambulance. They decide to keep her in hospital for a week until her "numbers" are better, and we have serious doubts that she has been eating properly or taking her medications on schedule because she is often asleep for long hours of the day.

Now my husband has to go over and check on Terry because we aren't really sure if he is taking his medication either or looking after the dog properly. When Chris arrives, Terry has locked the door and won't let him in. After some angry back and forth through the door, Chris gets a ladder and nearly plunges to his death trying to get his fat middle-aged ass through the upper bedroom window. There he finds that Terry has spread frozen tortellini and grapefruit slices all over the kitchen floor for the dog. Obviously he hasn't taken any medication for a while. He is on his bedroom floor eating cheese doodles and playing *Mortal Combat* on an ancient Nintendo system. When Chris finally pushes the door open, Terry starts yelling at him to get out of the house. He is a huge guy, and Chris has never seen him angry like this.

He decides to call his sister to confer on the best course of action, and they agree that they need to get the police to remove him and "section" him to the psych ward to get him stabilized. His sister and her husband come over to offer support. After a long discussion with the police at the front door, they finally convince the officer that they are the sane representatives of their mother's best interests, so the police call in special duty back-up with psych training. After a while, three more giant officers appear. After a long, tedious discussion with Terry, they end up carrying him from the house crying like a little baby. It is a very upsetting scene that no family should ever have to endure, but it is happening.

The next day, my poor husband has to retrieve the dog and drop him off at the SPCA to find him a new home. Shortly after this, my mother-in-law is placed in a full-time care facility near our home. Her kidney function stabilizes after a short time since she is finally eating and dosing properly. Chris feels a huge weight lift off his shoulders.

Back at our place, things aren't much better. A few weeks later, the alarm wakes us up again screeching in the middle of the night, and mum is actually in distress. She is sitting on the toilet with a pained expression and announces to me, "I can't pee."

"How long have you been sitting here for?"

"About twenty minutes and nothing is happening. It's painful. I can feel the pressure building up in my abdomen."

I turn on the tap as you would for a child, but this doesn't help. She agrees to let me put a Depends on her and go back to bed, but then she is clearly still very uncomfortable. An hour later she wakes us again using the "bells of doom," which are some old brass bells she jingles to call for help. She is moaning in pain and agrees to let me call an ambulance.

After we secure the cat in our bedroom, we watch them carry my frail old mother down the front steps straddling a seated back-board. This will recur three times over the next six months, as her bladder infections become more frequent. She has insisted that she doesn't want us dealing with her toileting issues and that this will be the final straw towards moving to a care home. We set up a commode beside her bed in the interim, but she doesn't like me emptying it in the morning. She feels embarrassed and hates imposing on us. I tell her it's not a problem every time, but it's becoming clear that we need to find a care placement imminently. The system requires us to set up home care for several months first, so we will have a woman coming in every day to empty the commode, wash and dress her and set up her coffee and snack.

After three months, Mum asks me suddenly one morning, "Why do I need these people coming in every day? I can get dressed by myself. I'm just really slow."

She has no memory of going to the hospital three times and denies vehemently that this ever happened, at which point I realize that her short-term memory is failing. I start watching her pills to make sure she is taking them, and the reminders become more frequent. I dread having the talk with her about moving into a care home. She might get angry and accuse me of being an ungrateful fifty-four-year-old child, even though we have been doing this for nine years now. I pray that my sister doesn't weigh in on her side and tell me it's unnecessary. *Maybe she should step up and put her money where her mouth is or butt out*, I think.

The cat dying is the last straw. The mangy old decrepit thing went out one night and never came back. After that, Mum couldn't take it anymore. She crawled into bed in the fetal position, feeling way more morose than when my dad died. She emerges three days later and finally agrees to the care assessment we have been discussing. I coach her not to make things sound all rosy and wonderful or she won't get onto the wait list for a subsidized residential bed. At ninety-three, god knows she has been paying taxes long enough to deserve one. She worked full-time throughout my entire childhood.

When the case worker arrives, I pull her aside for a private conversation. I try to impress upon her that my husband and I are feeling fairly fried after nine years and that Mum doesn't remember all the trips to the hospital. She seems sympathetic to our cause, but you never really know.

Mum answers all her dementia quiz questions—what day it is and who is the prime minister is—rapid fire, so this won't help her qualify. However, her physical impairments seem fairly obvious once the case worker asks her to move around the house. She can't carry things from the microwave and should not be lifting a kettle. She can't bathe herself or get to the phone, and sometimes she needs help just standing up from her chair, so it's fairly obvious to me that she needs full-time care. But who am I to say?

This lovely case worker leaves us hopeful after an hour and a half of meddling and tells us we have twenty-four hours to accept or decline a bed and move her in should we get the call. No pressure.

So, after a few days, when Mum is in a happy mood, I broach the issue of preparation. She once again denies that all this is really necessary, but I persist as cautiously and tactfully as I can. She finally agrees to let me sort through her clothes and shoes with her and find out what's essential and what can go to charity. She allows me to bag up the items that are out of season. On another day, I approach toiletries in the same manner. I decide not to get into the household knick-knacks with her, as this would create an endless sea of troubles. I will make a command decision when the time comes, as I'm sure the space will be very limited.

I realize how lucky I am to have a mother who has allowed me to plan ahead. We have already done the will, power of attorney, representation agreement and "Do not resuscitate" order. We have already divided up all her assets and antique household treasures between my sister and I. We have already minimized her carbon footprint by giving away her car that she can no longer drive. Most adult children can't even broach these topics with their parents without fear of conflict. My mum has been a rock of stoic practicality à la Winston Churchill since forever, and I only hope I can be as decent with my children when my time comes.

When we do get the call a month later, Chris and I are out driving. We pull over to talk safely when we see the number on my screen. Miraculously, we are offered a bed at the care home closest to our house and right next door to his own mother's facility. We cannot believe our luck, and we immediately accept. We are sitting in the car looking at each other gobsmacked. Suddenly, all the possibilities of living on our own flash before us. Travel, entertaining guests and even daytime sex become options. Letting the garden grow over into wild disarray seems like the obvious first order of business. Getting rid of fifty-year-old ceramic clowns and decorating the place in our own style will be delightful. Listening to the Cranberries instead of Frank Sinatra and the Tijuana Brass will be a welcome change. Even though I love my mother to bits, the whole world becomes new and exciting in that one phone call.

When we get home, Mum surprises me by accepting her fate with grace. I was expecting a huge fuss and some tears. She allows me to pack up her things, and we choose her favourite armchair and a small bookcase to organize her necessities, like her TV snacks and lotions and stationery, within reach. We even agree to bring the full-size electric piano along shortly with a rental truck so she can continue to play every day.

The next day I am expecting tears on all sides, but we are all surprisingly calm and efficient. Once she is settled in, we accompany her to her first dining room meal and meet her table mates. She has clearly been placed at the lucid table because all the other tables are what my mother-in-law calls "the drooling zombies" who require feeding and have no idea where they are. There are some real characters at this table, with a retired teacher from the remote far north of BC, a Scottish woman who has travelled widely and a Puerto Rican centenarian with great-great grandchildren who grew up in New York.

After supper, we leave Mum to her television programs. She seems quite content in her new digs, and we cannot believe how easy the transition has been. Chris and I decide to go out for ice cream to celebrate our new-found freedom. We keep looking at each other with new eyes of disbelief, as if we just got married that day and we forgot to plan our honeymoon.

Chapter Two

The Second Honeymoon

S o begins the next year of massive transition. As a certified mama's boy, Chris retires early to spend more time with her before she dies. It ends up being the double house clearing of the century, as our siblings agree that selling both family homes is the best thing to do. There is a minimal amount of wrangling over heirlooms, since my sister and I have done this long ago, but Chris consults with his local siblings and comes to an agreement fairly easily, which is a godsend. His sister takes all the photos with the promise to make copies. She wants a few larger pieces of furniture, and he wants the roll-top desk. Jewelry is divvied up according to taste and equal value. I have to ask my adult daughter if she ever wants to read a box of my old love letters from relationships pre-marriage. She does not. Apparently there is a line, and this would cross it, so into the recycling bin they go.

The local charity shops are filled to the rafters with our bygone treasures. We are not sure who would want a heavy glass yellow ashtray from 1970 or a plastic cat clock whose tail flicks to the seconds, but somebody will. No doubt, some inspired businessman wanting to look the part or a drama troupe looking for costumes will even appreciate my dad's fifteen identical grey London Fog raincoats.

Then there is Chris' deceased stepdad Craig's workshop across town that is filled to the rafters with old European motorcycles and their obscure parts. He contacts an old compatriot from Craig's ancient Rolodex and tells him to take what he wants for a nominal fee. He then spends days online with collectors from the U.S. and finally secures a buyer who appears from Montana with a huge truck to take the rest. We use the cash to pay off his stepfather's credit card debt, so his mother is pleased. The work is physically exhausting, but necessary.

Thankfully, both homes sell quickly and there's enough money to pay for the mothers' care homes in perpetuity. I am able to retire early the following year as a result of the sale, which allows me to spend more time visiting my mum as well. We appreciate the blessing of being free to really talk with them and hear all the old stories before it's too late.

We are constantly on call to deliver care items they request. His mother constantly wants chocolate, and we are amazed she never has high blood sugar on her monthly tests. Mine wants fresh fruit, dates, walnuts, yogurt, low-sugar cookies and fresh-baked treats. Then there's the drugstore items that we must smuggle in. Pads for mild incontinence and extra stomach and pain remedies, which the doctor won't approve. We suspect Chris' mother is self-medicating with Gravol to fall asleep because they've put the kibosh on her four-a-day sleeping pill habit, but we figure that after eighty she can do what she damn well pleases. We feel like personal shoppers to the stars or a concierge service.

So, for the first time ever my husband and I are alone. Our children are both living out of province. We move into a new townhouse, which is an uplifting fresh start for us. We whittle our stuff down to a bare minimum in the process of purging our parents' homes, and we enjoy choosing a new place and decorating it without all the ancient knick-knacks of our childhood. Once settled in, we take a long look at each other and say, almost in unison, "When did we get fat?" The house is eerily quiet and empty, and we know that if we don't find something to do besides watching TV together we will become like those giant people they extricate from the house with a harness suspended from a crane because they can't be lifted by any human means.

The psychological impact of retirement creeps in. Every Sunday night we get stressed out as if we are going back to work on Monday morning. When Monday comes, we feel the euphoria of realizing we really don't have to go in. We can sit and drink coffee and read the news or do a crossword as long as we like. Friday nights have lost their mojo completely. There is no mini-celebration at the end of the workweek and no alcohol-fed burnout session. Weekends become just another couple of days. When the first pension cheque arrives in the mail, we cannot believe we are being paid to do nothing.

Then there's the guilt. Every time we talk to a sibling or a friend who is still grinding it out, we feel sheepish. We cannot say anything about how great it is not to have to wake up to an alarm every day. In fact, we are now automatically on call if family members need help with odd jobs like loading a truck or driving a relative to the airport. If one partner is still working, then their partner should be doing every household chore and have a nice meal ready for them when they get home. That's only fair. Chris did this for me for my final year of work, and it was such a treat to come home and not have to cook dinner for us and Mum.

After retirement, the day disappears in a flash, and we wonder how we ever got so much done. Now it seems like whenever we run into an old buddy, they offer us a job. The guilt makes us wonder if maybe we should still be working part-time to bring in a little extra cash. We still feel physically able, and we kind of miss the camaraderie and feeling of relevance work provides. Even though the pension cheques always run out by the end of the month, we don't really need the extra money, and we'd rather be writing or golfing. However, this nagging feeling continues for about a year. Chris occasionally still announces that he is bored and wants to get a part-time job. Then I remind him how much he loves to wake up at five in the morning and watch recorded sports or poker on TV with nobody around and then go back to bed until ten o'clock. He quickly realizes this is true and gives up once again on this crazy idea of work.

So, we tap into our separate interests like you're supposed to if you want to stay married and avoid murdering each other. I join a writer's group and begin to write my first novel. I take painting classes and golf lessons, increase my gym time and go on daily nature walks. He joins racquetball and billiard leagues, returns to golf after a ten-year hiatus and reconnects with his cousin's family who now live close by. We begin enjoying daytime sex (adult children cringe now) and are still very attracted to each other after all these years. We take turns cooking dinner, which we both enjoy. We spend too much time playing mindless computer games. At night, we watch European murder mysteries on Netflix and cuddle our cat. It is a blissful existence of sleeping in and reading or writing over long, drawn-out coffees. Retirement is sweet, and we might just be the two laziest people on Earth.

We have intentionally chosen a place to live that requires no gardening whatsoever because we have both been forced to maintain our parents' gardens against our will for a lifetime. We love seeing the landscapers arrive every Thursday to cut the grass and pull the weeds around the strata complex; it's some kind of small wish fulfillment. We clink our coffee cups together, turn up the Latin salsa music and dance around the kitchen.

Neither of us is the slightest bit handy, so we welcome tradespeople in whenever the slightest thing goes wrong. The really high ceiling in the stairwell is just a frightening testimony to our ineptitude; what will we do when the lightbulb burns out way up there? Call the fire department? I adore my husband, but I shudder at the idea of him ever picking up a drill or a hammer to hang our artwork. I have seen enough crooked shelving and odd holes in the wall for a lifetime. I would rather do it myself when he's out of the house. However, for some reason he can fix anything to do with a toilet. I suppose, in this situation, he is highly motivated.

We listen to world music CDs constantly, having amassed quite a collection when we were caring for my mother because it was music we could all palate. We also have a huge record collection and a turntable but never get around to playing them for some reason; it seems like rehashing the past, and I suppose our tastes have changed. We no longer need Van Halen at volume ten to get amped up for going out to a party. It's sad that my Led Zeppelin collection is going to waste. We used to love to get high, lie on the floor listening and singing along to the lyrics on the album sleeve. We decide we should try this again, since marijuana has just been legalized in Canada.

We buy a little ganja from a friend of ours who assures us it's not too strong. After a few puffs each, we look at each other and start giggling, feeling like we are teenagers again. Chris starts talking really fast, puts on a Police album, and we are dancing around the living room having a wonderful time. Then a wave of cold fear passes over my whole body, and I am consumed by paranoia. What if our mothers needed help right now and we are too stoned to drive? What if the neighbours knock on the door and can tell we are high? What if the pot I just smoked reacts adversely with the medication I'm taking and I have a heart attack? My mouth is totally dry so I drink some juice, remembering the old adage that vitamin C will help bring me down. This is not fun for me anymore, and I decide I won't do it again. Chris seems to be enjoying himself but is way too hyper to act normal in any public situation. He is dancing around yelling at me about our inventory of spices and how his old friend Ronny is a grocery wholesaler and the Toronto Blue Jays might actually have a chance this year and he needs to get an oil change and isn't Sting a fantastic bass player? He sounds deranged. Maybe this was a bad idea. We get the munchies, eat dinner and crash early.

We realize we are sleeping way too much but we don't care. Sometimes we take two or even three naps in a day. This officially makes us old people, but we can't help it. Make a big breakfast? Nap. Go out shopping and visit the mothers? Nap. Entertain visitors? Nap. Go for a workout? Nap. Who cares what anyone else thinks? We worked hard for our whole adult lives and now we're lucky enough to be free of scheduled commitments all day, so why not take advantage of it? We are like cats, who apparently sleep seventeen hours a day, but we are happy. For the first time in our lives, we can do exactly as we please and it is wonderful.

Chapter Three

Our Grown-Ass Kids

The ultimate irony for any football-crazed, beer drinking, meat and potatoes kind of man is having a gay son as his only child. Of course, he still adores his son and supports him 100% in every aspect of his life. He says he already had a hunch when, at age four, Kiran ran around the bases the wrong way in T-ball and then asked if he could switch to figure skating. Initially, Chris was sad that he would never have grandchildren. Then he realized that, despite his previous beliefs, his DNA is not the greatest on the planet and he should really just get over it.

Now as an adult, whenever Kiran comes to visit, he always brings something to do because otherwise his boredom would be so intense he'd have to stab us to death right at the dinner table. He either brings a hectic board game involving picking up plastic objects really fast with chopsticks while some ninjas heckle you from a video clip, some strange vegan food he cooked or some CD of the most intense techno music ever. The music is nostalgic, though, because the repetitive thumping bass reminds us of when he was still living at home.

After a respectable amount of downtime, we try to eke out some details of his personal life, but this is like getting water from a rock. With us, he is not a sharer. The only way we have any idea what is going on in his life is through his stepsister's reports. For example, we know he was in a relationship recently, so when we ask him about it he says, "No, that's over. I am just being a slut right now." We then start to remind him to practice safe sex and he groans and tells us he knows all about that and not to worry because he is keeping up regular doctor visits. We get an update on his OCD medication and his roommate experience and then try to gently pry into his work life. He is in between careers right now and doing two part-time jobs while he decides what to pursue next. He wants to go back to school, and we have offered to help with this, but at age thirty-one the clock is a'tickin.

A year later, he has found his way into management training at the restaurant where he works full-time and is now in a committed monogamous relationship. For the first time ever, he is bringing his partner home from Calgary for the holidays. He is a lovely, gentle Vietnamese young man named Ken, who seems to perfectly balance out Kiran's hyper energy. We thoroughly enjoy having him stay with us. Ken even confided in me one morning that Kiran was too talkative when he got drunk and began oversharing at Xmas dinner while his auntie, uncle and cousin rolled their eyes at us and smiled.

A few days later we pay Kiran's rent because he has spent all his money buying everyone Christmas gifts and visiting friends. We drop them at the airport and hug goodbye for another year. We return home exhausted from a week of his draining energy and look at each other trying to figure out what the hell happened and where the time went. How did our children suddenly reach the age of thirty?

In the summer, our daughter Sonja appears. Her energy is much more calming, as she gives me shoulder massages every night and hangs with us just talking or watching funny movies. Her social schedule is also busy, but somehow less hectic than Kiran's. She also likes to catch up on self-care and sleep whenever she comes home. She sees a few old friends from high school and her paternal relatives, but nothing seems critical or urgent. We are constantly amazed she has been away from home for ten years, basically flying the coop as soon as she graduated high school. We have visited her in various locations like Nelson, Montreal and New Mexico where she currently resides. She is a jet-setter way more than I was, even though I consider myself to be widely travelled. She has even found a niche where she can work as a performance artist, which is miraculous. I swore I would never dissuade her from pursuing her dreams of doing a degree in fine arts after my own parents talked me out of music school.

She balks at the suggestion of ever having children as a heinous idea, even though her biological clock must surely be ticking at twenty-eight. There's a male friend she spends an awful lot of time with, but she keeps insisting that "It's not a thing, Mother." I keep encouraging her to let love into her life because she deserves to be adored. I'm worried that her bits will dry up if she doesn't have sex soon, after four years of ferocious independence and a long string of boyfriends starting at age sixteen. She seems focused on her personal development and her work way too much to be healthy. She meditates every day, eats a wonderful organic diet and goes hiking all the time, but she needs to get laid, in my humble opinion. However, she certainly doesn't want to hear this from me.

These grown-ass children show up once or twice a year and remind us they are actually self-sufficient adults, for the most part, other than needing a little money or advice from time to time. We still like to think they need us, but they really don't. However, we know from our own lives that we still value the security of our aged parents just being there as a port in the storm of life to turn to in case a crisis emerges. We still ask our ancient mothers for their insight into family relationships, gift buying, stain removal, taxes and, most importantly, crossword puzzle clues. Likewise, we are the security net for our own children, and we are satisfied with that. We think they are very lucky to have such supportive, non-judgmental parents, and they would probably agree.

I am jealous of my friends who already have grandchildren and can spend their days doting on them and buying them toys and sweet little outfits. However, it's apparently not always easy. Some of them tell me they get into pissing matches with their own kids for trying to parent their child differently than they do. One friend's daughter and son-in-law have become vegan and didn't want little Ben eating a ham sandwich, even though Ben loved it. The parents only want an hour of screen time a day, but Grandma is too exhausted to take him outside again. Meanwhile, Grandma is providing free childcare, meals and laundry service with little thanks other than the sweet hugs she gets from Ben every day. His parents look exhausted when they pick him up after work.

It's important to set boundaries with your own kids on what you feel able to do. It may only be one day a week of grandchildren instead of five so you can still fill your own life with fun activities. Just be honest and tell your kids that you don't have the energy to be a full-time caregiver or you really want to pursue your own interests and dreams after working for forty years. They will understand and respect you for it. You can always offer to help pay for alternate childcare for your grandkids if you're able to. Be generous, but don't be taken advantage of. Grandma and Grandpa deserve respect!

This last statement illustrates the cultural divide between us white North Americans and most others. For example, here in Vancouver, our largest ethnic communities are Chinese, Indian and First Nations. Grandpa and Grandma would always get the most respect. Elders would be included in the living arrangements in these cultures—it wouldn't even be a question. In fact, they would work tirelessly to bring the grandparents from across the globe to have them close.

White North American views on family have evolved into the current self-centred distancing of today. Most of us end up alone in care homes where, ironically, the staff are mostly people of colour. This arrangement allows these younger relatives to continue to work and play. I am not judging this as necessarily bad. I have grown up in this culture, so it is normal to me. However, I definitely see the value, both emotionally and financially, of the extended family all under one roof. The children learn from their grandparents, and the parents never have to pay for childcare. The elders feel needed and have support on hand. There are more working people to contribute to the high cost of living here, especially buying a home. The only sacrifice seems to be privacy.

So, Chris and I would love to have a grandchild soon, but with a gay son and a determinedly single daughter, it doesn't look promising. I have kept my Barbies for fifty years in the hopes of passing them on, but they may have to go to a needy family very soon. My husband would be the happiest man alive if he could play dinky cars on the floor all day, but alas, it may never happen. We will have to entertain ourselves. This is the ultimate challenge of retirement.

Chapter Four

Reaching Out

R etirement is terrifying for many people. We constantly run into friends who are close to retirement but cannot pull the pin. Of course, the first concern is usually money. Will they have enough to meet their monthly bills? But then comes a whole myriad of feelings. Most are afraid of boredom, especially men it seems. Women are better at social networking and maintaining friendships. They literally have a list of people they can hang out with and are more likely to initiate contact. The whole reason for women to get together is to see that person and talk. They don't even need to do anything; they can just sit and talk. For men, it's all about activities. The activity is the grabber; other men might show up for that activity, and that is just a bonus. If somebody else organizes the activity, even better. Then they can just show up and join into a familiar scene with other like-minded guys. The saddest thing I ever heard was Chris telling me how guys who had just retired from driving bus would show up back at the depot the very next day just to play cards and kibitz with the other drivers because they didn't know what else to do with themselves.

When you retire, everyone at your workplace immediately forgets you. As my husband says, you are just a payroll number who, no matter how great a worker you were, will be immediately replaced. He never has any rose-coloured glasses on in any aspect of his life, which is both healthy and cynical. I realize he is right and that if I wish to maintain any of the relationships I spent so many years building at work, I will have to diligently call, text and invite these people to visit, especially during the summer barbecue season when teachers are off work. I make a list of my most treasured friends, and one by one I contact them to get together. There are some who will enjoy nature walks like me, or meeting for coffee or lunch, and others who will prefer coming for a meal with their spouse. I am determined to keep these friendships alive.

I have three female friends whom I've known since high school. Two of them live close by and we hardly ever see each other, which is ridiculous. One of them works so much that we constantly worry about her health, but she seems to enjoy it. The second has a huge extended family that keeps her busy with births, graduations and weddings so she's hardly ever free. The third lives a ten-hour drive away, and I see her the most. We make a point of visiting each other a couple of times a year for a weekend catch-up, which is more like a therapy session because we know every detail of the past since grade three. She is the only one who always recalls little incidents from high school, like when the class clown streaked through the gym in grade ten or the most popular girl in high school broke her tooth opening a beer can at grad.

I also have some more peripheral friends whom I am determined to deepen my connection with. These are mostly work colleagues whom I made a strong connection with but rarely saw outside of work. Now that I'm retired, I have a chance to get to know them better in a social environment away from the pressures of the classroom. I have found a few rare gems of connection this way, since at work we never had the time to really talk on a deeper level about life, love, family, the things that matter. It has been really worthwhile digging out my old work directory and calling up the ones I felt a kinship with. On a staff of about eighty across two schools, there are probably fifteen women and just a few men who I really still care about. I try to set up a pub lunch with them at least once a year. They are all retired like me, and we are starting to sound old as we lament changes to the education system that allow kids to play on their devices all day. Why aren't they outside running around getting dirty like the good old days? Why are their parents making them ten-course organic lunches every day? We all got bologna sandwiches on white bread, and we turned out just fine! There is much talk now of grandchildren, chronic aches and pains and vacations abroad. Sometimes we hear ourselves and realize we are clearly out of the loop.

My husband is more casual. He values keeping in touch with a few men he worked with and chats with them mostly through Facebook. He has a few lifelong friends and then another few sports buddies through golf, racquetball and a billiards league. Like most men, his friendships exist around activities. They have to be doing something to interact with each other. God forbid they should just sit around talking, and going for a walk together is definitely unmanly. He also has the advantage of a large extended family who live all over British Columbia and keep in touch regularly. I have no relatives to speak of, having much older European parents whose relatives have mostly died, so I am grateful for his family being a part of my life too. They are a fun bunch of highly irreverent people who love to play games and talk and drink until the wee hours.

My husband also has one buddy from high school he has kept in touch with. His name is Bruce, and he happens to live very close by, so we rekindle with him and his wife. These friendships are so important because of the mutual reference points to our younger lives and funny stories that only they share. Who else knows that Chris was captain of the football team in grade nine and stopped a bully from pushing Bruce into his locker one day? It was this that created their lifelong bond.

Then there are the party friends from our twenties. They hung out with us at the same bar most weekends, and they might have even been our first roommates or college crew. They have seen us at our absolute worst: the walk of shame version; the puking version; the broke and desperate version; the naked version. Nothing has been left unsaid between us so we worry that some of these drunken secrets may come out without warning in front of our current spouses. They have embarrassing photos somewhere, which we hope will never see the light of day. We only see them once every few years when one of us makes the effort to reach out and reconnect, which is always a pleasant surprise. We meet for lunch, rehash the old stories and catch up on the havoc life has wreaked on both of us in the last forty years. We might share wallet photos (really dating ourselves) or cell phone photos of our family. Then we part with a hug for another five-to-ten years.

Chris' work colleagues from his twenties and thirties are also important to him. He worked in a warehouse for eleven years, and this period formed some of the tightest bonds he has. There are so many funny stories and weird expressions from this period that he quotes all the time; it's like they have their own secret language. If you "Tell Gurma Quick-a-Quack to go and get a can of sparks for the forklift," it means sending Sherman on a wild goose-chase. If you "Pull a Nick," it means you're going to take two porno mags into the boiler room on the night shift, jerk off and take a nap. If you're going to "Get ready for a meeting like Bobby," it means you're going to wear the loudest neon-coloured blazer you can find and put on a checkered tie. This is guy code's finest hour. There are literally hundreds of expressions from this period that my husband uses that nobody else understands except me and his old warehouse crew. He makes an effort to see these guys once or twice a year, usually at poker games. He really loves them.

At this age, if you want to make new friends, you need to join a group activity. For me, that is nature walkers, painting classes, writers' circles, yoga or Zumba. For my husband, it is always sports, billiards or card games. He has recently become interested in old cars, even though he hasn't got a mechanical bone in his body. Shamefully, he has bought gold-panning gear and a metal detector. This stuff is off-the-charts-crazy to me, and I do not want to be seen with him in public with him when he is using it. I suppose I should get behind whatever makes him happy, but I just won't appear in any photo with a man wearing waders.

When you join a new activity group, like my writers' circle at the local coffee shop, you never know who you are going to meet. Some people will immediately chafe; their personality will be so different from yours, and you will never see eye to eye. For me, this is the group member who tries to make me feel like I'm speaking out of turn when I interject during the welcome spiel. At my age, I don't like being shamed or put in my place for speaking. With others, you will feel an instant connection, like you've known them for years. This is the lovely Chilean woman with a beautiful, warm smile who is so welcoming to me. Then there's the majority, to whom you feel pleasant but indifferent. After the very first group, the Chilean woman invited me for lunch, but I made an excuse to go for my daily walk instead. After sitting for so long my back was sore. I came to regret this because she was the one person who I felt the most drawn to. It was a missed opportunity to make a new friend.

Occasionally out in the wild we even get to meet a young person! This is a rare treat because it makes us feel relevant for a brief moment. At writers' group this is the fresh face who is still at university doing her English degree and hoping to take the world by storm as the editor-in-chief of *Time* magazine. She is deferential to my age and wants to hear everything I have to say about my travels. She picks my brain for her upcoming trip to Europe with her boyfriend. It is adorable and flattering. I am suddenly reliving the days of my Eurail Pass and hostelling. She encourages me to write stories about these trips from forty years ago, which actually seems like a good idea. She leaves me in a reverie.

The next day, Chris and I run into a couple of our kids' friends at the mall, so we buy them a coffee and catch up. They are already married and expecting a baby. We can't believe that they own their own place already; our own kids are nowhere near that settled. We are amazed at how this young couple can earn enough working from home as graphic and app designers to afford a mortgage. The world of work is changing fast, and we are no longer a part of it. At least we can pat ourselves on the back for getting the references they make to current TV shows and music. Our own children keep us up to date on current media. I am techy enough and have even learned how to blog and use various social media apps, but Chris is less inclined. He wouldn't know a hashtag if it slapped him right across the head.

At this age, it is also time to let go of friendships that are no longer working for you. Some people in our lives have been toxic for years, and we have been trying to hold on to something that was never really there in the first place. Unfortunately, some of these people may be family members. Just because they are related or married into your family doesn't mean you are compatible. I barely saw my sister for the last twenty years of her life because she always blamed me for the way her life turned out. I couldn't take it anymore and had to let her go. It was a sad situation.

Some old friends might have developed substance-abuse problems. My husband is a rescuer by nature. When we are out in public, he tries to help anyone he sees who is struggling, whether it be carrying a pregnant woman's groceries or helping a senior get his wheelchair into the elevator. He has several friends who are alcoholics. He has tried to be supportive of them because he loves them, but they have sometimes been abusive in return. If one of you has been trying too hard to make it work, then it's probably futile.

Some old friend may now have mental health issues. My long-time girlfriend was suffering from PTSD, and she pushed me away every time I tried to reach out. She was delusional and paranoid, and she blamed me for spreading lies about her divorce, which was completely untrue. I eventually had to cut my ties with her. I have been waiting for an apology from another old friend for over thirty years, and I really need to let this go and move on emotionally. There's no time for hurtful relationships at this point in our lives. We all have regrets, but they should not weigh us down on a daily basis. Sometimes, writing a letter to the person who hurt you and then either sending it or burning it can be therapeutic towards letting go and moving on.

So, maintaining friendships post-retirement is a lot of work, but necessary to avoid social isolation. I often pause to reflect on how my life would be if my beloved husband suddenly died in a freak accident. This scares the hell out of me. There are so many lonely people, and I am determined not to become one of them. I'm not going to spend my day sitting at the mall scratching Keno tickets. I know I can't wait for the world to come to me; I must go out into the world and make connections. This is critical for good mental health as we get older. Aging is scary, but I will try to make the most of every day and stay as active as possible. It's not always easy, and there are often painkillers involved, but I will do my best.

Chapter Five

The Joys of Travelling

After retirement, we took a few trips abroad. Our idea of a vacation is mostly to lie by a pool in Mexico, get served free drinks and eat at five different buffets every day. I justify this by doing thirty minutes of water aerobics with the hunky Pedro every morning after breakfast. This burns off at least half a slice of bacon and keeps my heart from exploding.

I was fifty-six years old the first time I ever went snorkelling, a bucket-list activity. I managed quite well to avoid inhaling seawater or crashing into the rocky shore. I saw a few Mexican fish, but the water is not as clear as they show in the videos, so my vision was limited to a couple of metres. I was thrilled to have met my goal and also relieved that I didn't feel seasick at all on the boat. We drank a margarita and ate a fresh fish lunch on the ride back to shore, satisfied with the day's outcome.

My husband and I both loathe the idea of crowding onto a tour bus to spend an extended period of time with a bunch of strangers. Even on a seniors' tour, you know there will be personalities that clash, like Loud Drunk Guy who thinks he's still twenty-five and Oversharing Woman who thinks she's your best friend and never shuts up. Personally, I would rather go to one place on our own and stay there for at least a week to really get an authentic feel for it.

My dream city to visit is Barcelona, so we went in 2019. We also stopped in London to visit my only close relatives. It was nice to know that the cousins I had seen only five times in my life still instantly felt like home because of all the family history we share. There was so much to talk about and so many blanks to fill in. We loved sharing photos and telling the old family stories and were surprised when we heard a different version of the same story. We found that even across an entire ocean, we like the same foods, clothes and entertainment. There must be a genetic component to our tastes; or is it just passed down from the parents who grew up together as siblings?

Barcelona was spectacular, and we roamed every corner of the city and visited every museum for a week in glorious weather. We sipped delicious tiny cups of coffee and marvelled at the lavish pastries on every corner. We walked along the beach boardwalk, dipped our toes in the light blue Mediterranean and imagined we could see Africa on the horizon. We were amazed by Gaudi's architecture and Picasso's and Miro's paintings. We ate tapas and paella and sipped great wine. We were disappointed that the hot tub on the roof was closed and the one in the basement was tepid. We really wanted to dissolve our aches and pains after walking all day. The hotel bed was too hard for me, so I spread five pillows underneath my body, and this helped. The breakfast buffet was excellent, and we were located right in the heart of the action in the Gothic quarter, so life was pretty great. We enjoyed the hop-on/hop-off tour buses with open roof seating and the wind in our hair. By the end of the week we knew the bus and metro system enough to self-navigate. We felt like we knew our way around the city, and this is how we like to travel.

Now in 2020, coronavirus brought travel to a screeching halt. Everyone must stay close to home but, to be honest, we were starting to find long-distance flights and preparations exhausting anyhow. After COVID-19, we will probably prefer travelling within Canada and hopefully the United States too, if they also recover and regain stability. We would love to visit New Orleans, Maine, Boston and a few other cities. Chris' favourite aunt lives in Nova Scotia, so we could combine that with an east coast tour. We have talked about renting motorcycles (we both ride) and taking Route 66 from Chicago to Los Angeles. We have seen most of the west coast, but San Diego is on my wish list as well. We're hoping their next election will bring about some change, but I'm not counting on it. The rich still seem to be getting richer and the poor stay poor and medically uninsured down there. Where's the next Obama when you need one? Their two-party system seems to have failed them.

As travel restrictions lift a little in British Columbia, I'm focused on getting away to Tofino for a week this summer, which is my favourite place on Earth. My parents drove us there every year as children when you could only access it via a logging road. We would stop and picnic on hard-boiled eggs, buttered rolls and a thermos of hot tea beside the Taylor river, sitting on the rocks, and then we would continue past Ucluelet to some rustic cottage we rented on the beach. I remember gathering a myriad of beautiful shells and big sand dollars to bring home and display in the woven First Nations cedar baskets we bought locally. My mother gathered periwinkles, cooked them and dared me to try one. It was just like eating escargot, which does not appeal to any seven-year-old. Exploring the tidal pools created the most magical memories of my childhood, and my sister and I swam in the ocean for hours until we could no longer feel our legs. Once, my father had to pluck me out of the undertow as I nearly drowned. I can feel this memory right now with every fibre of my being; the panic, the relief of being rescued, and the unforgettable knowledge of the sea's power. No wonder this place left an indelible mark on my soul. I would live in Tofino in a heartbeat if my husband didn't object because it's too remote for him. I am determined to move to the seaside on Vancouver Island in the near future.

My lifelong obsession with the ocean cannot be denied forever. I feel such a strong pull to walk along the seaside every day until I die. I feel at peace when I'm there in such an inexplicable way. It's almost as if some past life regression is drawing me back to a birthplace I have never known. Don't tell anyone, but I secretly believe that I'm a mermaid. Perhaps it's because my mother was raised by the sea in England? I'm not sure. All I know is that it will be very difficult to convince Chris to move because he had a recurrent childhood dream of drowning in dark water beside a burning pirate ship. He has always had a fear of dark water because of this.

So, during the COVID-19 quarantine period, I become obsessed with looking at real estate over there. I spent hours finding the perfect location and tried to remain closer to civilization so that Chris will have enough amenities to play his sports and join a billiards league. He is a highly social individual, whereas I am becoming more hermetic as I age, like my mother. I was shocked that during the final year of her life, this formerly avid gardener wouldn't even let me take her outside at the care home in her wheelchair. She said she preferred to stay inside, but I think she was overcome by fear. I hope I don't become agoraphobic like her as I age, but it's a distinct possibility.

Chris longs to return to the Okanagan region of British Columbia where his grandparents lived. His fondest memories are of this hot, dry climate that is one of the fruit baskets of Canada. He can smell the cherry pies his grandma used to bake and taste the peaches he had to eat out on the stoop because they dribbled juice all down his chin. He would walk down to the corner store with all his cousins, buy a bag of penny candies and eat them all the way home. It was the thrill of a lifetime when, at age five, Grandpa drove him around the yard in a convertible Shriner's parade car. They would swim in the lakes all day and get freckled all over. This is where he wants me to move, but I long for the rainforest, not rattlesnake country. We are at an impasse.

I have always been a restless soul. I travelled a lot in my youth and had no fear of hopping from country to country on the trains of Europe and staying alone at youth hostels or with strangers who a friend back home connected me to. I sat naked in a hot spring under the full moon in Yellowstone, rode a horse to a waterfall in Haiti, slept in a cave in Turkey, seduced young men on trains and took them along for a few days. My life was exciting before I was a full-time working mother at twenty-eight.

Now I'm afraid of everything. I have anticipatory anxiety about boarding any type of transit due to a traumatic incident from my past. I was travelling in Europe when I was young, and I took an attractive young Norwegian guy back to my aunt and uncle's home for several days. Then, on the train into Amsterdam, he suddenly announced he was going to buy a brick of heroin that day. I freaked and almost passed out. I needed to get away from him immediately. Every fibre of my being was telling me to run, but his belongings were back at my relatives' home. I ended up paying a hundred dollars to get a taxi back because I had a panic attack and felt faint. He came back that evening, collected his things and left. I felt like a fool for misjudging his character so completely.

I have worked tirelessly to overcome this fear every time I board some kind of transit by using gradual exposure techniques. I even forced myself to take commuter rail to work for two years to kill the beast, but it still happens every time I go to the airport. Once, it was so bad that I went into the bathroom feeling faint and realized I couldn't feel my legs. I'm fine once I'm on the plane because I'm not afraid of flying itself; I'm afraid of missing my connections and all my plans unravelling in a great cascade of stress and disappointment. It's completely illogical, but it's real. I am thankful to have a partner who knows how to calm my nerves by saying all the right things and generally taking care of me. I take care of him by having a compass in my head and knowing how to read maps on GPS because he has little sense of direction. Together, we make a reasonably good travel team.

So, we shall see where we end up. Maybe we will get the courage up once again to go overseas. There is back pain involved in this decision as well, which is extremely boring. I would love to see Scandinavia and the Croatian coast, and Chris has always been fascinated by the ancient world and archeology, so perhaps Greece or Israel? My daughter is drawn to the Buddhist temples of Cambodia, so who knows? She always has the power to make me feel younger and take more risks, so perhaps I could still be drawn into another great adventure. Here's hoping.

Chapter Six

Losing Your Parents, and Siblings We Love to Hate

My wonderful mum survived for a year and a half after her placement in the care home and died peacefully in her sleep one month shy of her ninety-fifth birthday. That is a good long life by anyone's standards, so I cannot complain, especially since she went quickly and didn't suffer a long, drawn-out illness. She even had her mental faculties still intact, and we had a good conversation the day before she died. I am so grateful she died before the COVID-19 outbreak happened and started decimating local care homes.

I have heard so many horror stories of siblings fighting over inheritances and never speaking to each other again. I have several friends whose relationships with their siblings came to a crashing implosion after the death of their parents. One of my girlfriends told me her brother and sister emptied the family home, split up the possessions and sold it without ever consulting her. Two other girlfriends were written out of their fathers' wills in favour of their new wives who had just joined the family. They had to convince their siblings to "lawyer up" and claim back their birthright. Two other friends had to pay off stepsiblings they knew nothing about to make them go away. One friend's father had impregnated their childhood babysitter, and this love child suddenly appeared out of the woodwork to claim their due. Settling wills is often deeply divisive, and the wounds sometimes never heal.

Every family seems to have that one child who has always been the black sheep and wants a pity party thrown for them whenever they hit rock bottom. They might be suffering from mental illness, drug or alcohol addiction, or they are just socially inept and have never had a decent job or relationship or taken care of their children properly. They often live in their parents' basement well into their thirties or forties and are the drain that sucks up all the parents' money throughout their lives. When the parents die, they automatically expect to get the lion's share because they are so hard done by.

I probably sound like a cold-hearted bitch but ask anyone over fifty who that person is in their family and see what they say. You'll be amazed how consistent this is. I know that mental illness is very real and requires our support and empathy. I have less pity for people who won't seek help for their addictions, especially if help has repeatedly been offered and refused. Speaking from personal experience, most people fall into patterns of behaviour quite young, and most find it very difficult to change even if they are the one suffering the most.

Conversely, there is always the one sibling who takes responsibility for everything around their parents' care and estate. He or she does all this without being asked and spends hours talking to caregivers and lawyers and banks and tries to make sure everyone is provided for. This is the high functioning offspring who is typically blamed for the unfair divvying up of assets and then hated for the rest of their lives by all the other siblings.

This is me in my family. My sister and her children have repeatedly threatened me as thanks for doing everything. We split the house and valuables equally and have not spoken since. In my husband's family, he and his sister have shared the load pretty evenly; she does the paperwork, he does the grunt work like cleaning out houses and delivering essentials. It has worked out well, but the other sibs don't really understand what's involved. The one sibling in absentia for the last thirty years will undoubtedly reappear, suddenly wanting to be included as soon as his mother passes.

Do I sound bitter? Maybe I am, but no more than the average caregiver, from what my friends tell me. The high-functioning offspring take a lot longer to grieve because they are so busy dealing with everything. My husband and I had to madly box up everything in my mother's care home room as her body lay there awaiting pick-up by the mortuary. This was a strange experience for the books to be sure, but we are pragmatic people. It had to be done so we did it. My ever-stoic mother would have surely approved. The other siblings could wallow in their grief from a distance; we were not afforded such luxury. We drove straight to the funeral home and made all the arrangements. Then I slept in a chair at the funeral home while Chris unloaded all Mum's worldly possessions into our garage in the pouring rain, returned the borrowed truck and drove back to get me. The whole day was a complete blur.

Then came all the running around closing bank accounts and care home accounts, cancelling payments and memberships to every organization she belonged to, closing pensions, picking up signed copies of death certificates and wills, notifying all the friends and neighbours, placing an obituary notice in the newspaper, mailing cards overseas to distant relatives, making funeral arrangements and ordering flowers, arranging photograph displays, getting through the service, then thanking everyone. The final kicker was doing the taxes of my dead mother and still owing money to the government. After that, you can sit in a stupor and begin the grieving process.

I hope that round two of this with my husband's mother will be a little bit easier, but I know he will be a shattered mess and, just as I leaned on him, he will need to lean on me. It will be different yet the same. I will no longer be the paperwork queen, his sister will do all that, so there are some small blessings. They are also carefully planning for this eventuality with all the necessary legal paperwork.

Losing your parents is a mind-fuck. For the longest time you still think they are there and even pick up the phone to call them. It must be like the shadow limb of an amputee. You see an unfamiliar flower or hear a funny joke and think you will share this the next time you see them, but then you realize they are no longer there. It's repeatedly shocking. You hear them commenting on what you are doing as if they were right in the room beside you, but then suddenly realize that they are gone. It takes years for this to sink in and you feel more bewilderment than sadness.

Their passing is like taking a cold shower. After you get over the initial shock, you have to come to terms with a whole new reality that is both liberating and frightening. Your own mortality stares you right in the face for the first time, and you are forced to take stock of your time on this planet. You realize that if there are things you really want to experience or accomplish, the clock is ticking. You do the math and wonder if you might have twenty good years left, thirty if you're very lucky.

You have just suddenly become the elder in the family tree now. All the nieces and nephews and cousins see you as the old-timers, and you will be remembered by them as such, just as you remember and perceive your own aunts and uncles. In your mind you are still eighteen and relevant. You are the one who backpacked through Europe by yourself three times and skied down a glacier and got high and danced at an outdoor stadium concert. How can you possibly be this grey-haired relic that stares back in the mirror and whom little children call Grandpa or Grandma? Where did the last fifty years suddenly go in a flash? The whole thing is bewildering.

I truly hope that some of you manage to maintain positive, loving relationships with your siblings at this difficult time. They can be of great comfort in sharing memories of your deceased parent. After all, they are really the only ones who know the whole backstory of your life. But if it turns out that you're more like me and you feel a disconnect with your sisters and brothers, then I fully support you forging your own path forward. You do not owe anything to family members who try to drag you down with negativity, spitefulness or greed. Set your boundaries and be clear in expressing them. Learn how to say no when too much is asked of you. You are under no obligation to spend your precious time with relatives who don't understand, love and support you. Life is too short.

Chapter Seven

Reaching In: COVID-19

The COVID-19 pandemic forced us all to stay away from our friends and neighbours in May 2020, which meant all my great ideas about reaching out to join groups were moot. But I didn't despair. There are lots of creative ways to use the time productively and feel content, like writing every day, of course.

I could still volunteer at the cat shelter once a week, but we worked on our own and the public could only adopt a pet online and pickup from outside one at a time. Back at home, many projects awaited me that I had been lamenting for years that I never get enough time for. I decided to seize this opportunity to clean the garage, make a pile for the thrift store, recycling station or city dump. I cleaned out my closet and made a donation bin of all the things I don't wear anymore or my kids have left behind and will never use, like their scooters from when they were ten.

48

Inside my clothes closet, I couldn't help but pause to examine some of my old wardrobe. Getting older, you start to notice your own possessions in a different light. I realized I have many clothing items that are thirty years old, but they were still in good shape. I have so many memories attached to a particular piece that it became difficult to part with it. I wore that blue skirt to my wedding shower, the Pretenders concert and my daughter's graduation. I had overalls from my university days that miraculously still fit me (I bought them oversized). I will probably never wear them again, but how can I give them away when they are so cool? I rarely buy myself anything new because I deplore wastefulness and throwing useful items into the landfill. It suddenly dawned on me that I will die with this same wardrobe hanging here. I have recently emptied my deceased mother's closet and given it all to goodwill, and I pictured my daughter doing the same thing with my clothes. It is a sobering thought. I pitched as many items as I could part with into a plastic garbage bag for donation.

And what about all the photo albums from my parents? Will our children even be interested in them? Nobody under forty has room for such things anymore. Everyone is living in tiny apartments and other modular spaces because the cost of real estate has gone through the roof. This is a throw-away generation with no storage space. I decided to photograph them all, save digital copies for the kids and then throw them away. If you don't want to do this yourself, you can always hire a broke university student to do it for you—once they are allowed back in your home, that is. I asked Chris to chuck the old, yellowed family collection so I didn't have to feel the guilt and sadness. I made a command decision to open every box in the garage and remove all the frames from the photos first. There were at least a hundred of them just taking up space. I decided to hold a garage-sale-frame-give-away in our strata complex by donation to the food bank.

Before I took pictures of them to create digital files, I decided to make one old-time album for each kid. I enjoyed working on that for a while. I even decided to go the craft store and get some cute scrapbooking stuff to see what that's like. I discovered that every sticker and page and set of corners costs a small fortune. It's quite a racket. So, I half-assed it in my own pathetic way with a few beach stickers and cute, colourful corners until I was quite satisfied with the result.

I decided to try the hobbies I always believed I would enjoy, such as watercolour painting, planting a herb garden, building a miniature hobbit house and setting up a blog. Garden shops are still open and busier than ever, and they even offered an outdoor class for the hobbit house I want in the corner of my tiny yard. My daughter's painting teacher graciously offered to have me in her home for lessons since she has very few students over the summer. There are hundreds of YouTube videos showing how to undertake any new project I wish to try, and now I have the time to do them. And of course, I will write.

My husband's volunteering to drive the elderly to their shopping came to a grinding halt in favour of grocery delivery because it's safer for the clients. He likes to cook, so he started trying new recipes even though we are pre-ordering our groceries for pick-up, which makes it a bit trickier. He made some terrific curry and started working on a creamy stroganoff. He even asked me to add certain herbs to my tiny box garden on the patio, which he never used to care about. He bought a wine making kit and set it up in the basement. He has a buddy who is an expert, and they are chatting online about it.

To combat feelings of isolation while the gyms were closed, we went outside every day for a long walk, even when it was raining. It was easy to stay away from others by giving a wide berth on the trails. Just saying hello to people with a smile cheered us up, and it's okay to pet dogs because they can't get the coronavirus. We even rediscovered the pleasures of having a picnic. When the weather was nice, we pulled out our Tupperware, packed up sandwiches and fruit and drove to the nearby lake for lunch. It broke up the day and cheered us up to look at the mountains and see the odd bald eagle gliding overhead.

There were also so many ways to exercise at home in the living room during quarantine. We did some stretching after every walk, and once a week I went online to do Pilates and yoga with an instructor friend and a few other women. Chris wanted to stretch with some weight resistance, so I gave him two full laundry detergent bottles to use as part of his routine until we could buy some proper weights. Quarantine was the time to invest in that elliptical trainer (if you still had a pay cheque) or pull out the old rowing machine buried in the basement. People with home gyms were at a strong advantage since most of the local facilities were closed.

My husband and I constantly listened to music to lift our mood. We got used to playing feel-good mellow music when we lived with Mum, like smooth Latin jazz and electronic lounge music. Occasionally we will play an old record after dinner to wax nostalgic. I even pulled out my guitar and old song sheets, and we sang a few old songs together. I know it sounds cheesy, but it was fun and Chris loves karaoke, so why not? I downloaded a few new tunes we like so I could learn the chords. We really wanted to sing "Major Tom" by David Bowie.

I went online daily to check in with friends and relatives on Facebook to see how they were doing and have a chat. I became much more addicted to social media and even gained a lot of Twitter followers, some of whom feel like real friends. Expressing the same fears about this virus with others helped relieve our collective worries and realize we are not alone. We also called our elderly relatives who don't use social media to lift their spirits. Chris loves letter writing, so sent a few to the older aunts and uncles in his family to cheer them up. We have lots of blank cards and stamps in the house, so it was easy to do and made him feel good.

Before you start to vomit thinking we are this obnoxiously perfect couple, let me be honest. There were definitely days when we felt lazy and blue. We slept, ate and drank too much for sure and often found it difficult to get motivated to do anything before eleven o'clock. Our morning coffee and reading time stretched into ridiculous lengths. The cat was so spoiled during this time that she expects to be fed and fussed twenty times a day. She knew we were there to open and close the door for her whenever she wanted, and it got really annoying. She had us wrapped around her little paw.

There were times when Chris needed to get away from me for some bro energy. Thank god the golf courses and tennis courts were still open. He has one friend who lives on a big property, and he went there to chat at a safe distance and help feed the chickens and walk the dogs. It was a great escape for him. If I needed to get away from him, I usually headed to the local forest trails. We knew that spending too much time together could damage any relationship, and we can usually sense when each other need some space.

We were also aware that many people were really struggling with loneliness or, at the other end of the spectrum, violent relationships during COVID-19, and this is no joke. We saw the ads for the women's shelter hotline on Facebook and realized that living in quarantine with an abusive partner would be sheer hell. Never mind all the families with small children who were climbing the walls with boredom. Schools and daycares were closed, and those poor parents had to homeschool their kids and somehow earn enough money to pay their bills. Playgrounds were plastered with yellow crime scene tape, and they had to explain to their three-year-olds why they couldn't have a birthday party. We were so glad to be past that life stage during the lockdown. It must have been terribly difficult. The government was giving out subsidies, but they were never enough. There were so many people out of work and living hand to mouth.

Teenagers also must have been suffering terribly from this isolation since they are pack animals by definition. They must have been so immersed in social media that their parents wondered how they would ever function in the real world once this was over. Imagine being fifteen and in love and not being able to see your boyfriend. The fights that would have ensued between parents and their teenage kids during quarantine would have been scary. Even the mall food courts were closed, so where were they supposed to hang out?

Since most teenagers love gaming so much, we decided to give it a try. Maybe it would expand our minds and be super fun. Neither of us grew up with any exposure to this, but our kids are millennials, and we bought them games on the PC and a driving console. They mostly played *Mario*, *Sonic*, *Star Wars* and the like. Then they became the first *Pokémon* fans and played on their hand-held Nintendo DS consoles. We phoned our brother-in-law for advice on how to get started, and he recommended buying a PlayStation 4. Chris had always wanted to try *Grand Theft Auto* after laughing so hard he fell off the couch watching Conan O'Brien narrating his own game play. We also tried a few pro sports games, but we were absolutely hopeless. The athletes were mostly running around in circles. After a week of driving into concrete walls and traffic light stanchions, we gave up and returned the system for something easier.

Our bro said Nintendo Switch was easier, so we got some racing and sports games to try. We were much better at this but found the games too juvenile by the end of a week and finally gave up on the whole idea. Gaming is just not our thing. We don't get it. We have no interest in exploring fantasy worlds to try and kill off imaginary villains. We missed the bubble or maybe we are just too old and have maladaptive brains. We sold the console and games to a happy father of two and moved on.

On a more serious note, we watched the news every day to keep abreast of any new provincial recommendations for personal and community safety during the pandemic. This made us feel like we were part of something much bigger than ourselves and told us what we could and could not do when we left the house. We were trying to remain hopeful that it wouldn't last forever and to do our part to keep others safe.

We even started chatting more with our neighbours over the back fence and keeping a safe distance. We swapped a few items with them, like cat food and eggs from our friend's farm, and they picked up prescriptions at the drugstore for us because they are younger and didn't have as many health risks. We even posted a note on our strata message board to see who could trade us some used jigsaw puzzles for Chris, with great results. These exchanges would not have happened if it weren't for this virus, so there was some sense of community building here, which was positive.

Unfortunately, things were and are terrible in the United States. Hospitals were overrun, and the number of deaths hit one hundred thousand. Then George Floyd was killed by police in Minnesota, and most big U.S. cities erupted in violence. Nobody out protesting seemed the slightest bit concerned about social distancing. It's as if coronavirus had suddenly been pre-empted by the Black Lives Matter movement. Everyone was asking where the leadership was because their loathsome President Donald Trump had yet to make an appearance on TV asking for calm as most major cities were being burned and looted. It seemed he was more concerned about his Twitter profile. It was very discouraging to watch, even as a Canadian. My daughter lives in the States and we are all human, so it felt very close to home. It was a sad situation.

In some other countries, the coronavirus outbreaks drastically improved in May as governments around the globe enforced "stay at home" orders to curb the spread. Italy, China, South Korea and Russia were examples of such controls working positively, as well as here at home in British Columbia. We didn't know how long this was going to last, and everyone braced for the fall/winter flu season. Staying home in the rain and snow was much more challenging for people, especially if they lived alone or needed assistance.

The care homes in BC were still on lockdown and struggling to keep their patients alive. COVID-19 mostly killed the elderly here in BC. Most of the nurses and care-aids in our mothers' facilities are Filipino, and they are so lovely, gentle and kind. We are grateful to them for immigrating here to look after our elders. Many of them have left their entire families back home, some even left young children across the Pacific in the care of grandmothers and aunties. How worried they must have been for their own loved ones, yet they were caring for ours every day without complaining. It was really astonishing.

It seems like young Canadians see this work as either low-paying or gross, and they don't want to engage, even though the demand is high. Apparently, our culture does not favour elder care. Everyone is too self-absorbed with trying to get ahead and make the almighty dollar. I have to admit, I would not have wanted to change seniors' diapers when I was in my twenties either. Now that I have done it, I know that it's just part of the lifespan coming full circle. I have cared for my own mother like I cared for my baby; it's the same thing. You just do it automatically out of love.

After a few weeks, things started to open up a little. Parks reopened and even public washrooms were available, which made a big difference if you were travelling longer distances by car. Children were allowed to climb on playgrounds again, and schools reopened on a rotating schedule. Children attended only two days a week, and many opted out since it was only for the month of June. Online learning continued for children aged twelve and up. Within weeks we were allowed to travel within our own province for summer trips.

However, the border to the US remained closed. This was a wise decision because things were much worse right next door in Washington State. There were, on average, five hundred new cases per day there, and in the worst states, like Florida, five thousand. The rioting continued, but it was gradually simmering down. I worried about the impact of all the protest gatherings on the hospitals that were already overrun. It's the poor nurses and doctors who are left to pick up the pieces. I worried about them catching the virus and not having enough staff in our hospitals. Also, their mental health will be impacted. How many of our health-care providers will suffer from PTSD after this is all over? Who will replace all the caregivers who need to go on leave to look after their own health?

I have been spiraling down a rabbit hole of negative thinking and must stop myself.

I have tried not to think about the refugees and war zones that are also dealing with COVID-19 because it is really depressing. Instead, I made a donation to the United Nations Humanitarian Coalition for Refugees and this helped me to feel a little better about it for a short time. I hope this will all be over soon and will become just a historical case study in how to better manage future health crises. We all wait for a vaccine to emerge before too long that will save humanity from this pandemic and return us to normal life.

Chapter Eight

Giving up the Battle of the Bulge

At some point you will say to yourself, "Why, at almost sixty years old, do I still beat myself up every time I eat a potato chip or a pastry?" You will look in the mirror and say, "To hell with it! I have been fighting my body my whole life to try to maintain a shape that has now become unattainable." You might even make a conscious decision to give up, enjoy yourself and turn off that little nagging self-critical voice. I'm not saying you will start eating only junk food and stop exercising altogether. It's just that you shouldn't care what other people think of how you look anymore. My mother used to always say that people only think about themselves and don't even notice how you look. If you ask the person you visited yesterday what you were wearing, they will have no idea.

I gave away all my work clothes to the local thrift store and to a couple of women friends who are my size and are still working. I realized I never needed to wear dress pants and collared blouses again. It was liberating, and I am looking forward to wearing my hippy dresses and tracksuits for the rest of my days. I might even wear velour occasionally like George Costanza. I will definitely be comfortable. I used to put on make-up every day for work, but now it has to be a special occasion like a restaurant dinner or party. I will not primp and preen for a trip to the store. Hell no.

Maybe you've always wanted to change your appearance but were too scared because of your work setting. Now you are free to explore and get that makeover with pink hair or that long dreamt of tattoo or piercing! Your family will be amused, especially the kids or grandkids. They will think it's cool and suddenly want to take a photo with you as the cool matriarch/patriarch. Unless, of course, you're a man and it's a mullet.

With all this free time, you also might start to notice your idiosyncrasies, and not in a good way. Like why have I been standing in front of the mirror examining my scalp for moles for the last twenty minutes? What was that noise I just made getting up from the couch? Why am I collecting plastic bags and folding them neatly into a fabric catch-all in the cupboard? How can my husband stand to watch me blowing my nose every morning at the kitchen table? I'm getting grosser by the minute, and god help the care-aide who has to deal with me when I'm eighty-something. It doesn't bear thinking about but, nonetheless, that's what I appear to be doing. I have been married to my wonderful second husband for twenty years, and it suddenly hit me that in another twenty years that the odds say one or both of us might not be here anymore. This is the shocking reality that motivated me to make the most of life right now.

When friends get together at this stage of life, they invariably start talking about their ailments.

"I can't do this because this hurts, and I can't eat that because it upsets my stomach."

Nobody wants to hear about your medications unless they have the same issue. Stop telling random people about your colitis the first time you're introduced. It's a bummer, literally. Save those discussions for friends who are close enough to you that you know some of their health secrets. It seems to be open season out there for surgery talk over lunch, which makes me feel sick to my stomach. Filter people—filter!

Women are worse for this than men. Men tend to hold their cards close to the vest. Women will talk about anything. They will tell you their breasts are sagging, their periods are sporadic, their insides are coming out, or they peed their pants on the way over to see you. Men, on the other hand, specialize in talking about shit. They will tell you what kind of dump they took this morning or if they are going to take one right now. Women are embarrassed about shit. They'd like you to think they never do it, and if they do it's only tiny pristine nuggets that make no sound when they hit the water. Most women have never farted in a restaurant and then laid claim to it with pride. This is men's territory. If they don't lay claim, it's a lost opportunity for status. I'm not sure if finely-dressed businessmen and lawyers do this as well, but I'm guessing they do.

At this age, it's time to become a realist. We all wish to be the athletes we were in our twenties, but it just ain't happening. I was a runner until my body decided, at age forty, that this was no longer an option. My feet hurt for years, and the only solution recommended by two different podiatrists was to shorten my second toe via surgery. No thank you. Finally, a third podiatrist said, "You have flat feet; you should have never been a runner." Ah well, that seals the deal then. Too bad, buddy, because I loved running for twenty-five years.

Now I walk every day instead. I love being out in nature, so I'm on a quest to discover every forested trail in my local area. I love knowing the details of my surroundings, which way each arm of the river flows, all the good swimming holes and duck ponds. I even bought myself a can of bear spray to be safe because my hubby was constantly worried. It's Canada, after all, and there are definitely cougars. The bears around here don't like humans much, and I'm outside of grizzly territory.

Chris hates nature walks. He thinks they're a complete waste of time. If it's not competitive, he's not interested. It's an interesting psychological phenomenon. I am a loner when it comes to exercise. He is a team's guy. I enjoy working out alone at the gym so I can relax and pace myself and get into that Zen space. The warm-down stretching to chill music is the best part for me. He loves to bro out and smash a racquetball back and forth until somebody gets hit and comes home with a round war welt on their skin. He will even play loud rap music in the car on the way there to get amped up. Even at this age, it means bragging rights, and he is happiest when the other guy is swearing loudly because he is losing. That keeps the testosterone elevated enough for him to feel good for days.

In between nature walks and gym workouts, I ache all over. My lower back, hips, hands and feet are the worst. I am constantly using an icepack or heating pad, icy-gel roll-on pain reliever, and I'm taking way too much ibuprofen. The idea of taking a big trip seems overwhelming now; just sitting on a plane is physically painful. We both function well in short bursts of activity and then we need a nap. Sometimes we nap two or even three times a day. I have come to the conclusion that we are getting old, and it sucks!

The medications on the kitchen table are impressive. We have a fantastic doctor who has known us for twenty-five years, and we believe in science. We will take whatever she recommends. We are not inclined to try gluten-free, dairy-free or meat-free diets or natural alternatives to modern medicine. We are stubbornly old school. I know I take too much ibuprofen, but my doctor is not concerned about it. We have managed thus far to avoid the three big ones: high blood pressure, sugar and cholesterol, so we feel relatively lucky. I'm in the borderline range for the latter, so I'm getting checked more frequently and watching my intake of fats. This is all very boring, but typical for our age. We are painfully normal.

A lot of our friends have gone back to cannabis for various health reasons. They are smoking, vaping, eating gummies, taking drops of CBD oil or rubbing it on their skin. In Canada, it's recommended for so many ailments and mood disorders. I tried drinking droppers full of CBD oil for a month for my arthritis, but it didn't seem to help me. Perhaps I needed a higher dose. I know several people who have beat cancer and swear by the stuff as a pain reliever. They say it worked miracles in their hour of need. Maybe I need to try a different strength or eat the gummies, but I'm afraid of my anxiety kicking in again. I could probably talk to the pot shop staff and get a more relaxing strain that would also help my chronic pain. My husband still smokes occasionally, and it makes him a little hyper, but in a fun way. He likes using it while playing golf to help his game because it gets him out of his head. It's good to be open-minded and try new things.

But no matter how much exercise we do, it never seems to make a difference to our size and shape. Chris laments having his grandfather's body with a hard, round belly, and I lament having my mother's soft, flabby stomach that never disappears no matter how many sit-ups I do. We embraced each other's physical shortcomings long ago and often say, "We're fat and we're good with that," as a cry of capitulation and acceptance. I have ugly veins in my legs, but I'll be damned if I'm not going to wear shorts outside when it's hot. He has weird skin tags popping up all over the place. The scars of time are rapidly increasing, and we know we cannot win. We know it's better to accept them and take solace in the fact that everyone else is going through the same changes. We will use our physical abilities for as long as we can and try to feel grateful every day.

The trick is to keep moving. Even my ninety-four-year-old mother tried to walk a lap around the care home with her walker until the last six months when she was wheelchair bound. Otherwise, the body slows down and forgets. Whenever I tried to help her with routine tasks she'd always say, "You must let me do as much as I can, even if I'm painfully slow at it." She was right. We tend to jump in and want to take over as caregivers, but if they can get dressed by themselves, let them keep this sliver of independence, even if it takes half an hour.

We also have the time now to appreciate the beauty around us. That's why it's important to feed our souls by going to concerts and visiting art galleries, museums and gardens. Read the classics, dust off your musical instruments, plant some flowers and try new recipes. These are all expressions of joy and sensual gratification. Of course, sex is nice, too, so enjoy it whenever you can. Take extra care in the details of setting the mood with candles, scented oils or toys. Talk to your doctor about erectile dysfunction medication or hormone therapy if you need a little help in this department. You might just be pleasantly surprised by the results. Don't be afraid of buying lube or a sex toy to spice things up. If science is allowing us to have sex later in life, take advantage of it. The improvement in your mood and well-being is totally worth it. Then you can think of your partner with a twinkle in your eye when you're out at the mall having coffee with a friend, just like in those cheesy TV commercials for Cialis.

When I spend time with my children, I am more likely to try new activities. Younger friends can also motivate us to step outside our comfort zone, and we many even surprise ourselves. I recently hiked along a river trail to a remote hot springs with my daughter and her friends, and it turned out to be the highlight of my whole year. Normally, I'm the least daring person ever. So, if you get the opportunity to join a younger group, grab it and hang on tight, even if it's a little scary at first. Be clear in explaining any physical limitations you have before you go so they can make adjustments for you.

There are all kinds of community groups at the local rec centre or seniors' centre.

I recently tried a Tai Chi class, and all the Chinese regulars made such a fuss over me. It was very sweet. They introduced themselves and laughed when I didn't know where to stand. They pulled me into the centre of the group, this giant blonde woman in shorts and runners towering over them and making all kinds of mistakes, but they seemed thrilled to share their culture with me. It was a lovely form of movement and surprisingly challenging. I was tired after the first hour and had to say goodbye at the break. They were all much older than me, and they were staying to do a second hour, so they were all very fit.

If you're daunted by group fitness, then start by following some yoga or Pilates videos at home to get back into movement and stretching gradually. If you have a little extra money, you can hire a personal trainer or physiotherapist to set up a gentle program and show you some exercises at home until you feel comfortable enough to go to the gym or rec centre. These professionals are used to working with all levels of fitness, from completely disabled or recovering from injury to people in tip-top shape, so there's no need to feel embarrassed if you're overweight and/or out of shape.

Remember that your health is a combination of all these things. We are past the age where body image should worry us anymore. We are all lumpy and saggy and imperfect. Try to get out occasionally instead of staying home all the time. We are meant to be social creatures, even if we are shy by nature. Taking small steps to improve your strength, endurance and mobility will enhance your quality of life and give you more energy. If the group you're looking for doesn't exist in your community, start it yourself! You can ask your local librarian to advertise it for you if you're not good with computers. You can ask at the local rec centre or seniors' centre to find you an instructor for hire and book you a space, and then you can charge members a small fee to pay for it. I guarantee there will be like-minded people for anything you're into.

Chapter Nine

Volunteer Work

After mourning the death of my mother for six months, I decided it was time to give something back to the community from my place of relative privilege and idleness. But where do my passions lie? I am instantly drawn to the elderly after all the caregiving of the past decade, but something in my gut told me I needed to avoid that for a bit. I tend to think like an older person already, so I decided to explore younger pursuits for the time being. Also, I'm afraid that every old woman I see will remind me of Mum and make me start crying. It's just too soon.

I am absolutely potty about cats, and I love visiting the local shelter so why not start there? Spending time there is a win-win because it picks up my mood and helps all these abandoned creatures. I have been scooping up cat shit my whole life, so it's no big deal to clean litter boxes, wash and refill food dishes, give them medicine drops wearing the protective eye goggles and long leather gardening gloves or vacuum their rooms.

There are plenty of them who love a good scratch while I'm there, and I know which ones are chatty and will have a full conversation with me talking cat language in my crazy high voice. Even if I am not fit for human company, I speak fluent cat. My only real challenge is not taking them all home with me. Our place is quite small, and we have one kitty who hates everyone except me, so she would not tolerate any other cat joining the family.

One day, a man came in with a mother cat and a box of kittens he had found holed up in his barn. They were the most adorable hungry little things I've ever seen. The mother began to eat ravenously, and we called the vet to schedule their intake check-up. I immediately started thinking up names for them. I name the ginger male Conan, the black female, Wanda, and the black male Chappelle.

"Oh, you can't name them!" a colleague scolded. "Then you get way too attached and you will be sad when they are adopted. Besides, the family coming in will want to choose a name themselves. You have to call them one, two and three."

This sobering reality shut me up. I prepared some clean bedding for them in a box and plopped the babies on top of their mother, who had finished her meal. They all nuzzled in and found a teat. They had to be kept in a separate room until they were checked by the vet, and then only with other females until the mother was spayed about two months later. I felt happy for the rest of the day that this little fur family was rescued and would go to loving homes.

My husband told me he wanted to get involved in helping others as well. He told me about an old lady he had seen pulling one of those nylon grocery totes. She could barely walk so he stopped to help her. He gave her a ride home and carried her groceries up to her apartment. The next week he gave her my mum's old walker, which I totally supported. He loaded it into the trunk with her groceries and drove her home again. She was thrilled with the walker and tootled into the elevator pushing it along and looking much more stable. She wrapped up a few homemade shortbread cookies for him and thanked him for all his help. He left the apartment beaming with pride and feeling wonderful.

He found out that all the apartment buildings on that street were for seniors only. The seniors' centre is right beside her building and they offer activities and services for the community. Suddenly he had the idea that maybe he should be driving other seniors around to get their groceries and medicine on a regular basis. He explained this over dinner that night, and I was thrilled.

"Yes! You are so good with the elderly. This is definitely your true calling."

He began volunteering at the seniors' centre as a driver for five elderly people every Tuesday to do their grocery shopping while I was at the cat shelter. He was excited to get started the following week.

The first one was Mrs. Ross. She was tiny and Scottish with a thick brogue that Chris could barely understand and tried to imitate, to uproarious effect. Her only son died in an industrial accident, so she just had her little wiener dog, Rupert. He marvelled at the quantity of cookies she bought every week. They were mostly Peek Freans biscuits, and Chris lamented that she should at least buy decent cookies like peanut butter or chocolate chip. I told him she is probably diabetic and watching her sugar or perhaps those biscuits reminded her of home.

Chris' second client was Mr. Davis, an obese man who had the worst greasy comb-over Chris had ever seen. He came from Texas but married a Canadian woman who died ten years ago. He only listened to country music and talked non-stop about sports, which Chris quite enjoyed. His weekly grocery order always included seven big bags of Doritos and two cases of Lucky Lager beer.

The third pick-up was Mrs. Gauthier who hailed from Quebec City and still had a strong French accent. Her two daughters were back east, but they visited her once a year. She lamented having no grandchildren and blamed her two sons-in-law for being too selfish and weak to bear any children, never mind what her daughters may have wanted. She had a huge, fluffy Himalayan cat named Coco that she brushed every day to perfection. Her grocery order always included a can of Spam because her husband was a clerk in the Canadian embassy in Fiji for a while, where they got used to eating this staple.

The two o'clock client was Mr. Gable, who was so frail that Chris suggested he stay home and have the groceries delivered, but he insisted on getting out. It took ten minutes just to help him in and out of the car. Chris pushed the collapsible wheelchair while Mr. Gable pointed to the items he wanted. They loaded up a small, portable basket several times and transferred the goods into a shopping cart. Every time they got to the cashier, Mr. Gable wanted to pull out his cheque book and Chris had to remind him that he had to use the fancy bank card now. Luckily, he trusted Chris with his PIN, so the transaction didn't take a week.

His last client of the day was Mrs. Doyle. She was a loud, fat woman from the Maritimes who grew up in a tiny fishing village. She got mad every week when Chris reminded her that she cannot smoke in his car. She always complained that the fish at the deli counter was subpar and ended up choosing a can of sardines instead. She lamented that her son was a useless alcoholic who could not hold down a job and wouldn't fork out the money to come visit her.

Chris loved re-telling these stories when he got home.

"They are going to die you know," I reminded him.

"I know. I am preparing myself for that eventuality," he promised.

"Then somebody else will take their place and you will get to hear a whole new story," I said, trying to sound a little more positive.

"That's the part I like," he said. "Even if they're cantankerous as hell, they all have had interesting lives, and I always learn something surprising about them. Like I am picturing Mrs. Gauthier wearing a grass skirt in Fiji and dancing on the beach. Not bloody likely."

He always made me laugh when we shared these stories. After telling a tale, he would lean back in his chair, sigh and say with amazement, "Other people's lives."

****

On a more serious note, some people really have a burning desire in retirement to make an impact on a broader scale. These people are usually politically minded and feel all the injustice in the world deeply. They may wish to work on some global issue that's dear to their heart, such as poverty, famine, drought, social housing or human rights. Retirement offers the time to devote to a particular organization of their choosing to try and make the world a better place.

I have one friend who runs an orphanage in Kenya for children whose parents have mostly died from AIDS or conflict. She is affiliated with a church back in Canada that does regular fundraising to support her work. She has been doing this for years with her husband and loves her life and the daily spiritual fulfillment it brings.

Another retired friend went to Guatemala recently to take a month-long Spanish language immersion program where she stayed with a family in their home in a very impoverished area. The language program brings money into that community through the local school. She was so moved by the experience that she would like to go back for a longer stay and try to help the community with their fundraising and development efforts.

A man I know, who is a retired engineer, volunteered with Engineers Without Borders to build wells in Africa. Another guy who worked with my husband went to help Habitat for Humanity build shelters in Puerto Rico after

Hurricane Maria in 2017. Admittedly, these types of commitments require good overall health and may not be suitable for many of us. But they are surely rewarding and noble pursuits.

If you are more of a homebody, then you may wish to participate in local campaigns for organizations you believe in. I am particularly drawn to Doctors Without Borders (MSF) and The United Nations Humanitarian Coalition for Refugees. Their work reduces human suffering worldwide. You can choose whatever is important to you and donate your time to making phone calls, email campaigns, or you can tap into whatever strengths you may possess. Who knows, you could end up ordering or boxing supplies to be shipped overseas or designing their web page.

Whatever helping role you might decide to take on will make you feel like you are giving back something to the world in your own small way. I strongly encourage you to give this some thought. Retirees, not just youth, are in a unique position to change the world.

Chapter Ten

My Restless Spirit

wo years into retirement and living in a brand-new home, you wouldn't think I'd already become restless, but such is my nature. I admit I have a fascination with real estate and a constant desire to move, which is part of my lifelong desire to live by the sea. As it happens, real estate on Vancouver Island is generally lower priced than around Vancouver so I'd been watching it for a while and worrying that prices would rise and I'd miss an opportunity. Chris still really wanted to go back to his childhood haunts in the interior, but I think he was almost resigned to "Happy wife, happy life." He had been less resistant to exploring the options with me at any rate.

During COVID-19, Vancouver Islanders didn't want to see mainlanders on their island for fear that we city folk were carriers. However, after four months we were allowed to travel within BC so that was our chance to go over, look around and walk on the beach.

We booked a little four-day motel excursion and called in our lovely local cat sitter to look after Hazel.

COVID-19 restrictions meant we had to stay on the ferry car deck and wear a mask for the ninety-minute crossing, but it was totally worth it once we checked into our cute little hotel. I headed straight out for a walk on the beach. The wild Pacific filled my soul with joy as the pungent smell of seaweed filled my lungs. I was back where I belonged. Chris even admitted that it was beautiful and he understood why I love it there so much. However, he was reluctant to leave his golf, racquetball and billiards buddies permanently, even though he would make new friends instantly at any sports facilities because he's so friendly.

We went for coffee at a funky little cafe in the village of Qualicum Beach and grabbed a local real estate paper. I was in my glory circling two-bedroom condos on the ground level with a little grass for my cat. At this point of our lives, we don't need anymore space than that. I thought about all the crap in our garage that I would have to get rid of and wondered if I was really going to cart around the family heirlooms for the rest of my days. Do I really need an antique wooden tobacco canister? Probably not, since I don't even smoke, but it was my great-grandfather's, so it ended up in storage with fifty other oddities. How do you get rid of the things that your parents attached great importance to? Chris is much better at it than I am. After his mother went into the care home, he brought in an auctioneer to collect anything he thought would sell. This was a smart move, but one I couldn't stomach. So here I am, stuck with my great-uncle's top hat and cane for no good reason.

We circled a few properties to drive by before lunch and set our GPS. I fantasized about living in a mobile home. They are so cute and tiny, with a community feel that would provide instant social connections. However, the monthly fees are quite high; it's almost like having a mortgage, which is something we definitely didn't want. Chris convinced me this was a bad idea if we wanted to leave an inheritance for our kids. Some people don't care about this, but we do. Mobile homes decrease in value quite quickly and have a limited lifespan. Also, the land is most often leased from a property owner, so there is no land value. He gradually talked me out of it as we headed up the Island Highway.

We realized we could live in a seniors only building and wondered if being surrounded by older people would prematurely slow us down. It would be nice to have some amenities like a hot tub or a pool table and community rec room to meet people, but we also value our privacy, so it was a conundrum. Did we really want our neighbours knocking on our door to come play pool when we're having a nap? I wasn't so sure. I would rather go out and meet people on my own terms away from my sanctuary, but Chris is more social, and I don't want to cramp his style.

We were both hardcore realists at this point. We knew that an elevator in the building was an absolute necessity as we age and lose mobility. We knew that underground parking was important for safety and we didn't want to shovel snow anymore, which is apparently the number one cause of heart attacks in Canadian men over fifty. Our children hate to hear us talk this way. My daughter won't even hear me call myself a senior without cringing and protesting vehemently. I told her I'd joined the seniors' centre and showed her my membership card to prove it, but she just shook her head and insisted I wasn't old. Naturally, she wants me to live forever. Our aches and pains will not decrease over time; it's a purely mathematical truth, so we want to make the best of it and keep on exercising and exploring as much as we can.

We continued our morning drive, stopping to admire a potter's home studio with a sign on the roadside. An old hippy with a long grey beard, woolen socks and sandals emerges. He was smiley and apparently loves receiving visitors. He told us he had lived there since 1978 and would never consider leaving. He loves the quiet solitude of the oceanside and knows everyone in the village. He trades services for pottery. A woman repaired the lining in his coat in exchange for a shiny bowl, and a guy replaced the broken side mirror on his truck for a serving platter. Barter is still alive and well in these smaller communities. We purchased a set of candle holders and bid him good day.

We stopped for lunch at a pub where they served pan-fried oysters, which I love. Served with a pint of the local brew, we are in heaven. We sat on the patio overlooking the sea, and it was a cool, sunny day. Bundled up in a sweater, Chris was throwing French fries to a seagull, much to the waitress' chagrin. I asked him if he could see himself living here, and he began to relent. I got a long "maybe" in response. I was thrilled.

After lunch, our buzz was dampened by the couple who run the local bakery. They told us it's almost impossible to find a doctor around here and it's a thirty-minute drive to any hospital. Hmmm, this is not great news. We both have health specialists we need to access on a regular basis, never mind a GP. Perhaps half an hour is fine for scheduled appointments, but what if there's an emergency? Our cautious realism kicked in and we wondered if we needed to live in a larger town. We decided to head up the road the following day towards Courtney where they have a big new hospital.

We spent a lovely afternoon reading on the beach with a travel mug of wine and napping in our folding chairs. It was the off-season so there were few people around; it was pure heaven. We woke up groggy and headed back to the hotel to find a cup of tea. After a delicious supper in of local Coho cedar plank salmon and organic greens, we watched some Netflix foreign murder mystery on our laptop and crashed early.

The next day, we drove north to Courtney to look around. We found many beach access points, which was a big priority for me. I went online and found two rec centres with racquetball courts and a pool league in this town as well as several golf courses. I could see the wheels turning in Chris' head, but he kept asking, "What's wrong with where we live now? I love our home, and it's right by the forest for you. We have good friends there." I couldn't deny that we lived in a beautiful suburb, but I reminded him we needed to free up some cash for our retirement by purchasing a cheaper home. He reluctantly agreed this was true, but, unfortunately, the ocean only reminds him of his scary childhood dream. Am I a mean wife for asking him to follow me to fulfill my lifelong dream?

Every time we arrive back home, I realize we do have a lovely place, and I am probably being too pushy. I should respect his wishes since he is the best husband in the world. But I couldn't shake this restlessness to move again. Is it out of boredom? Was I not doing enough to make my life feel complete? I realized there was probably no rush, and maybe in five years Chris would slow down on his sports and be ready to move to a more senior-friendly small town. I just wanted to walk on the damn beach every day! Is that too much to ask? Marriage is a constant push-pull of dreams and desires, and I was in a quandary.

Chapter Eleven

Nostalgia

ave you ever seen that group of old men at the mall every morning sitting around the lottery counter playing Keno? My husband tells me they are there because they need their bro time away from their wives. He knows a bunch of retired men from work whose wives have literally kicked them out of the house every morning because they want their alone time to watch their talk shows or have a friend over for coffee or do yoga naked on the living room floor. Whatever it may be, it seems important to spend some time apart during the day or you will wind up killing each other.

The other function of this bros'/girls' time is to wax nostalgic about the good old days when you were relevant. Guys can talk about sports stats, politics, WWII, car parts, scrotum chafe or whatever else relates only to them. Women can talk about menopausal weight gain, sagging skin and body parts, shopping, children and grandchildren. I realize these are horribly stereotypical subjects, but you get the idea. You can't, and shouldn't, bore your partner with every detail of your bullshit or there won't be a hint of romance left in the union. That's why we seek out these safe sharing groups.

When our kids were teenagers, they rolled their eyes whenever we talked about the past, but then around age twenty-five, they suddenly started listening. They could not believe what we had lived through. Our lives seemed so strange compared to theirs. They wondered how we knew so much trivia when we played games after the holiday meals, and we told them we knew because we were there. We remember the top news items from the time when they actually happened.

We love waxing nostalgic because it takes us back to a time that was not necessarily better, just younger, healthier, and collectively familiar. There is comfort in sharing memories with others because it makes you feel connected and normal. It's amazing how many times we reference high school. I would never have believed that those teen years would still seem so formative and important to who we are now. It seems like a great time in our lives because we were doing so much and meeting so many people without any of the worries of paying bills or feeding ourselves. It was carefree in that sense but traumatizing in another.

I still recall the overt bullying and generalized fear I felt all through high school, and I wasn't even a total geek. I was just an average kid. There were known gangs in different neighbourhoods around the city and reports of fights in local parks at night-time. I was told you couldn't walk through certain areas alone because that one tough guy or girl everyone had heard of lived there and he/she would beat the crap out of you. I still don't know if there was any truth to these stories or if they were all just urban legends, but I was scared. I have talked to other people about this recently, and it was definitely a generalized phenomenon.

Our parents had no idea what we were up to or that we were afraid. Luckily, I had an older sister who was cool, so she shielded me from some abuse. I remember a known tough girl grabbing me in the hallway between classes and pulling me outside between the buildings where she was smoking with the toughest guy in our school. They offered me a drag, and I took one to look cool. An evil smile spread across the tough girl's face, and she said, "You're Rachel's little sister, right?" When I confirmed this, they looked at each other knowingly and decided to let me go. It was a terrifying incident. When I got home, Rachel told me she was good friends with the tough girl's older brother so that's why I got off scot-free. Nobody reported these incidents to the teachers or principal because they would have to face the scary person again in the office, and things would only get worse for you afterwards.

Drugs and alcohol were everywhere. My sister did a lot of acid, MDA, mushrooms and speed with her friends, and she tried mescaline and bennies (uppers). Thank god she drew the line at heroin; actually, it wasn't even really mentioned or around our suburbs in the seventies. She was promiscuous as hell, and it was a miracle she never got pregnant. Of course, she smoked pot all the time and introduced it to me when

I was eleven. I was a really academic kid who played sports and music, but I did enjoy smoking weed. We all smoked cigarettes as well. I was way more straightlaced than my sister, but she was exceptionally wild and didn't care much about school.

Chris and I also reminisce about our twenties and long for the energy and enthusiasm for life we had back then. At one point, he was working three jobs and playing on two different ball teams. I fondly remember working part-time while going to university in Montreal, taking the metro and walking everywhere. I was constantly meeting new people and going out to bars and restaurants. I felt omnipotent, like I could do anything I set my mind to. It was the most wonderful, interesting time in my life. I sat around with my three Jewish roommates talking politics, listening to great music and drinking 'til the wee hours. I took Spanish lessons at the local community centre and met a bunch of Latinas in the neighbourhood who threw great potluck parties with lively dancing. On the weekends we'd go to the Haitian dance clubs, a drum circle on Mount Royal or walk down to Chinatown for some hot and sour soup. We were only responsible for ourselves, so life was easy.

I think as I'm aging, I miss the excitement and adrenaline of my youth, but if I'm really honest, there was a lot of drama and emotional pain during those times. I took so many risks, suffered heartbreaks, incompatible roommates and worries about paying the bills. There were cheating scandals, STDs, pregnancy scares and close calls. My mind seem to selectively forget whatever caused me distress, and I only remember a golden time of endless possibility. This is why nostalgia is such a wonderful sensation.

However, when my husband and I reflect on our thirties, the sheen comes off the apple. We clearly recall the pain of our first marriages and the stress of providing for our young children. These were our most difficult years. We were often exhausted, broke, overworked and disillusioned with our relationships. So many of our friends got divorced like we did. That's when the bitterness set in and life really began to suck. Looking back, it's a miracle our kids turned out so well through all this bullshit. We managed to hold it together even when it felt like the wheels were coming off the cart. There is only nostalgia for how beautiful and innocent our children were during that period. Everything else about that decade was difficult.

Things got much better in our forties. We came together and moved happily into our second marriage, which has turned out to be the right one. Our children bonded, successfully became step-sibs and even liked each other, which was a huge relief. We were excited to fall in love again and move in together and create this whole new family. Things got easier because we both always worked full-time and could therefore pay our bills. As our kids moved from elementary to high school, we were still extremely busy driving them around to all their activities, but there was a lot of joy and laughter. Their friends were always in our home, and their various stages of development amused us in different ways. We gave lots of advice and set lots of boundaries. We fought with them and made up. We photographed all their milestones and shared them with the grandparents. There is plenty to be nostalgic about from this period.

Every parent our age knows that when the kids move out it is very sad. You don't realize it at the time, but they are generally not coming back, except maybe for a holiday or in between jobs. This is when you start taking a long look at yourselves and wonder what happened. This is when the real nostalgia begins. You miss your children terribly and try to suck all the good marrow out of the bones of your life. You reflect on all your accomplishments and mistakes and hope that the tally ends up in the plus column. For some people, it is especially difficult to look in the mirror and see that time is indeed passing mercilessly quickly. For others, there is satisfaction in knowing that your kids turned out okay and pretty soon, if all goes well, you will be able to retire. Here's hoping that you find yourself in the second group, having avoided or overcome the barrages of alcoholism, drug dependency or mental/ physical illness. We have lost some friends along the way, so we are not wearing rose-coloured glasses. For some, nostalgia can be a cursed longing for better times gone; I hope that for you, it is the gift of savouring all the good times.

Chapter Twelve

Keeping up with Technology

S ome of us older folks love the idea of having every new gadget, and we even have some money to buy them now that our living expenses have gone down. I want the latest fitness watch that counts my heart rate, steps, distance and generally warns me if I'm going to drop dead in the next thirty seconds, but I have no idea how it works. Even if I read the instructions, it takes me about a week to get the time and date set and to know which button to push for any given data.

Our grown-ass children really don't have time to help us with our technological ignorance though. They are always running from their job to their social life or yours may have children of their own with endless lessons and practices to get to. We remember what it was like to be this busy. We are left to desperately fumble around trying to keep abreast of technology, and our learning curve always feels steep.

Even though we have enough time on our hands, our brains absorb more slowly than they used to. I have busy Twitter and Instagram accounts and a blog website, but the latter only came with much swearing and many webinar tutorials. It felt like I was swimming upstream the whole time. I have seen school children absorb in five minutes what it took me a month to learn.

Teenagers say Facebook is for old people, so, of course, we love it. It keeps us in touch with old friends from every part of our long lives. We can even check out those whom we have lost touch with from a safe distance and then reach out with a shared memory if we are feeling brave. It has become an absolute lifeline for my mother-in-law in her care home during COVID-19. We cannot visit her, but we can send her photos and jokes daily to lift her spirits. We chat regularly with all Chris' relatives from his huge family to keep up with all their house moves, job changes, new babies, weddings and funerals. For anyone who is isolated, social media can be very uplifting.

I was encouraged to join Twitter as a new writer to gain a following in order to promote my first novel, which was scheduled for a year down the road. The result is that I'm now addicted and spend way too much time chatting every day. I feel like I have friends all over North America, Australia, India and the UK (English speaking countries) who are writers like me. We do not stick to the subject of writing; we talk about our personal lives and try to make each other laugh as much as possible. I feel like I've been sucked down a rabbit hole, but I'm happy inside. Some tweeps openly admit that these daily chats have literally kept them alive during COVID-19, with its social isolation bringing bouts of depression, social anxiety or simply feeling trapped with their kids at home for months on end. The importance of these connections is no joke.

On the lighter side, my husband and his buddy just bought metal detectors. When he told me he was going to do this I laughed so hard and told him I would never be seen with him using it. I encouraged him by saying he would strain his back carrying it around for three hours to find some old rusty nail and a 1964 dime. I wished him luck, as the supportive wife that I am. I was impressed he was able to read the manual and assemble it himself. The pair of them tootled off into the wilds of our town and came back happily exhausted with little to show, but they had a nice lunch out together afterwards and got some exercise, so that's all that matters.

I bought a GPS device for my older car and attempted to load all the current maps into it. There was much swearing as I tried to locate and read all the tiny serial and model numbers on the box. I realized then that I needed new reading glasses. Chris laughed at me and said we should just use his car whenever we travel because it has the GPS built in, but I wanted my independence to go on small road trips by myself occasionally, especially if he's still doing an annual golf excursion with his old work buddies.

We still have all our old record albums from the seventies, so we bought a decent turntable a few years back. Now we need a new needle for it. Luckily, Chris is adept at finding things on eBay. We have bought cheaper printer ink cartridges for years from Asia, cheap golf shirts and a case of the pain roll-on medication for my back to save money. I even got his retirement gift on there, which was a used gold chain-link bracelet he wanted. Finding deals online is his technological forte so I'm grateful for that.

For everything else computer related it's all me. My job as a teacher kept me on top of all the changes in hardware and software enough to be a fairly competent and consistent learner. I do all the online forms and registrations and manage all our personal documents and devices. I enjoy doing this, so it's not a problem, but I regularly try to teach him the basics so if something happens to me, he will be able to function and find all our info. He would struggle mightily, but he would have the good sense to ask his sister for help or figure it out.

Then there are the photographs. I have so many files on my computer in different folders and drives—some are in the cloud, some are in Dropbox—and it becomes an organizational nightmare. I need multiple flash drives to store them all, and then I can send some to be printed if I want hard copies.

We are both useless in terms of fixing and building anything around the house, other than toilets. For some reason Chris is a master at fixing toilets even though he can't hang a picture straight to save his life. I famously tried to put an IKEA bookcase together once and ended up in tears because when I was finished half the shelves were upside down. We cannot change the oil in our cars or tune up a bicycle, and we watch our neighbours out tinkering and admire their abilities. We would rather do the *New York Times* crossword or write a book. To each their own strengths, I guess. Too bad it ends up costing us a lot of money hiring others to fix our wares.

We live in a time when movie theatres are about to become obsolete. We can watch everything on Netflix or regular television streaming networks. Our friends marvel that we still listen to our CDs every day. Most people use streaming services for music now too. However, they always admire our record collection. Apparently, vinyl is back in vogue, so all our kids' friends want what the albums we bought decades ago. We were amazed to learn that some of these albums are selling on eBay for $30-$70 U.S. each. Maybe it's time to sell them and take a small trip within BC?

Chris still wears a watch, which is really archaic. I gave this up when I stopped working. We still use a wall calendar and keep takeout food menus in a drawer. We still keep our old invoices and records in accordion file folders. Hell, we still have a box of DVDs and cassette tapes in the garage that will no doubt end up as landfill. This throw-away society depresses the hell out of me. I have to stop myself from dwelling on where it all ends up. At least we have electronics recycling in our city. When visiting the U.S., I was appalled to learn that many American cities still don't have curbside recycling programs or green bins for food waste. Every company that sells stuff should be responsible for recycling their own products and re-using as many parts as they can. The environment is going to hell in a handbasket.

Recently with the COVID-19 pandemic, every service has gone to online booking. At the gym I saw older people—even older than me—asking for help on how to figure the booking system out. It must be so daunting for people who have no tech ability whatsoever and who live alone. Chris' mom lives in a care home, and we are not allowed to visit because of risk of transmission. Thank goodness the nurses are setting up FaceTime visits on tablets for the residents. People who are isolated can talk to their doctors or get virtual counselling support if they have the technology. Once again, poor people with no devices and no training are left out in the cold. There is a dichotomy of technological access that separates the rich from the poor and permeates every aspect of life now.

Back at home, we are hunkered down mostly self-isolating but getting outside every day because we live in a mild climate. We are connected with others and entertained by technology. I have recently switched from reading paperbacks to digital books. I've finally given up on the idea that it is nicer to hold a real book in my hands, which makes me sad for no good reason. We move forward more and more reluctantly as we age, sometimes dragging ourselves kicking and screaming into the modern age. I just hope my old brain can keep up.

Chapter Thirteen

Self-Care

R etirement is the time to decide if we are going to maintain our personal grooming rituals from our days of work or let our freak flags fly. We can try to go back to previous versions of ourselves or even opt for a complete makeover to reinvent ourselves.

Men can add various hairy features to their faces, such as a big seventies moustache, a beard or a nineties soul-patch. Some even opt for waxing their moustache into a point and wearing bow ties. Whatever makes you happy. We only ask that you investigate your nose hairs occasionally and buy a set of trimmers.

Most of my women friends have stopped wearing a bra around the house. This is always surprising for the Amazon delivery guy and not always in a good way. It's extra special when we haven't shaved our armpits for over a week, as in most of the winter. We can shower today or not; it depends what's on the calendar. If we booked the gym for tomorrow, then why not just wait until after the workout? We don't want to dry out our hair with too much blow drying right? And what about all the bikini line ceremony currently in vogue? Do we buy into the young girl's obsession with having everything neat and tidy down there or, even more impossible to maintain, completely bald? Or do we stand firm on our generational full bush pride? If we have a partner, he or she may weigh in on this, take it or leave it. I'm personally opting for some kind of middle ground to keep everybody happy. No creepy little girl va-jay-jay here. I don't even like those hairless cats.

Clothing-wise, there are so many choices to make or ignore. I tend to be a bit of a minimalist, living mostly in shorts, sweats, T-shirts and tank tops. I donated all my work clothes to the charity shops, but kept a selection of summer dresses, mostly loose and hippy-style of brightly-coloured Indian cotton, perfect for menopause and comfort. My daughter has ridiculed me numerous times over the years for wearing socks and sandals. I have never worn heels because I have flat feet and chronic back pain, which is not hot. I am less formal than most women and dislike shopping, so I guess I'm a bit of an anomaly. I can't imagine how women deal with their shoe collections from work after they retire. Do they keep all the high heels? I guess most of them have difficulty parting with their treasured outfits, but I do not.

I have just stopped the daily make-up regimen of my thirty-year teaching career. I look after my skin by washing my face every second day with gentle soap and water and applying a moisturizer with SPF because I'm fair skinned. The cream goes on as thick as spackle because my skin is so dry it instantly absorbs everything, even in summer. I will only apply make-up for special events, like a dinner party or a show.

As for the non-esthetic treatments available, I have to admit I love getting a massage on a regular basis. There is nothing more wonderful than getting flattened like a pancake for an hour by somebody's strong elbow. I highly recommend it. Once I even found myself in a Thai spa in Vegas, and I didn't realize that Miss Thang was going to climb up on my back. I let out a cry of pain and told her emphatically NO because it hurt like hell. I don't understand how people can handle that. I also tried the float tank sensory-deprivation experience, but it made me feel hot, dizzy and uncomfortable. My daughter loves it. I spend enough time with myself in the dark already, but I get why it's a popular trend. We are all so over-stimulated in today's world of endless media connectivity that it's good to check out in a silent pitch-black room every once in a while.

I have never had a facial or a manicure in my life so I can't comment on it other than to say that I'm too cheap to fork out eighty dollars when I can clip my own nails and wash my face in two minutes; always have done. Likewise, with colouring my hair. I have always bought a box from the drugstore and done it myself. Why spend $160 when I can do it for fifteen? I have always been very frugal, perhaps due to my parents' no-nonsense wartime survival mentality. However, I do understand why people like to be pampered by a stylist, especially if they've formed a confidential relationship with them. For some people it must be almost like going to a therapist.

On a more serious note, seniors are more injury prone, and many of us have put out our backs and shoulders doing something lame like pulling a weed or lifting a box off a shelf. I know that many readers do not have any physio coverage, but if you can afford a few sessions, I found it really helped me to learn the correct at home exercise techniques to fix my last injury. It takes a little dedication to follow through, but it's totally worth it.

Part of self-care is also realizing and accepting there will be days when you feel like doing nothing but lazing at home. Your energy cannot be high all the time, and this is normal. Don't expect to be going out every day. Indulge in quiet time like reading, writing, playing games, napping or taking a bubble bath. My husband loves spending hours doing the *New York Times* crossword puzzle, and I can happily get lost in Twitter. If you suddenly realize it's dinner time and you haven't even got dressed, don't beat yourself up about it. Turn off that self-critical voice and be grateful you don't have to go to work anymore or drive in commuter traffic. You are the one people envy now.

People my age also need to keep up with medical screenings. In the past two years, I have had a colonoscopy, an esophageal scope, a bladder scope, a mammogram, an ultrasound on my lady bits, a CT scan on my lower back, an ECG, a dermatologist's mole screening and regular blood tests. I am lucky enough to live in Canada where all of these are free, and I have an excellent female doctor. I fear that most American readers may not have these options available to them without paying through the teeth, but I hope I am wrong. I know there's such a wide spectrum of coverage down there that no two people seem to have the same level of support. It is baffling and discouraging. If you possibly can, at least get a doctor's physical once a year and take your medications regularly. I wish you all the best in your quest for good health care.

Let's talk about the Big C for a moment. I personally know at least fifteen people who have recovered from cancer and, unfortunately, a few who did not, including one of my ten-year-old students. There isn't much worse than attending a funeral with your entire classroom of kids. I honestly don't know how these oncology doctors and nurses can cope with the emotional toll. If you find yourself with this diagnosis, please take heart in knowing that more people recover now than ever before. I have so much admiration for my friends who have gone through chemo or radiation therapy and come out the other side with a new appreciation for life. They are some of the strongest, most positive people I know, and they generally appreciate every visit, every minute, every moment. If you receive a cancer diagnosis, please ask for help from your inner circle or from volunteer organizations like the local cancer society. There is plenty of help available across many areas of daily life, such as volunteer drivers, shoppers, people who deliver medical supplies and peer support groups.

What I'm saying is take care of yourself now that you have time. Be gentle with your body on a daily basis. Take a longer shower and enjoy the feel of the warm water on your back. Pamper yourself. Put candles around your bath or rub essential oils on your skin. Brush your hair for five long minutes just because it feels good. Spend a half hour stretching every morning. Cook healthy meals. Meditate, do yoga, go for long nature walks, read, relax and enjoy a longer morning coffee ritual with some music playing. Cuddle your pet or your partner more often. Take a nap without feeling guilty about it. We have all rushed around for most of our lives. Now is the time to take it slow and celebrate every day of your freedom from work.

Chapter Fourteen

Reunions

Now that we are of a certain age, we will probably be invited to all sorts of reunions for high school, college, the workplace and family. Chris and I may balk at first and think these people don't hold any interest in our lives anymore, but then we get this nagging feeling in the back of our minds that maybe we should go. We worry that we got fat and wrinkled so people will be disgusted by our older selves.

Then we start flipping through the photos on the Facebook invite. We are shocked to see that everyone we remember from high school looks ancient! How did they get so old? We suddenly realize, like a slap in the face, that this is how we look to them as well. Oh my god, do I look that old too? It becomes clear that we are all in the same boat. Who knows? Maybe we'll reconnect with that one person to whom we really felt a connection but never got a chance to exchange numbers with until it was too late. Maybe we will get a chance to show those popular jerks that they are no better than us and that their lives turned out just as shitty and normal as ours did. Who knows, maybe the prettiest girl in class turned out to be a raging childless wrinkled unemployed alcoholic? Fun stuff like that.

So, we should definitely pay the fifty bucks and go see the big show. We might never get another chance to glimpse into our past like stepping into a time machine. Will our prior predictions have materialized? Will the class nerd be a successful scientist or programmer? Will the jocks be selling used cars? Will the stoners be auto mechanics and truck drivers? Will the cheerleaders be stay-at-home moms with no careers? Or are these stereotypes no longer valid in today's modern society? It will be a fascinating study in human development.

When we arrive, there are always coolers full of local beer and a shitty rock band playing old cover tunes. If we're lucky there might be a few good food trucks and some tables and chairs. We are probably in the local hockey arena or some church hall or even in the old school gym itself. Everyone dresses as cool as they possibly can and wears a name tag. The same friendship cliques reconvene immediately into a safety net to chat about the good old days, ogle the passers-by and gossip about who they notice. Did you just see Julie Mitchum? She got really fat! Did you just see David Scarborough? He is totally bald now! Can you believe Mark Andrews and Carly Sawchuck got married? They have four kids and own that mini-golf place off the highway. Did you hear that Steve Williams died in a motorcycle crash last year? How awful for his wife and kids. Did you ever know that the gym teacher, Mr. Lewis, was sleeping with the drama teacher who was married? How did they not get caught during the five years we were there?

We secretly hope we will run into that one person who did us wrong and say something to clear the slate. For me, it was my best friend from age four to age eleven who suddenly dropped me like a sack of wet dog shit in favour of a more popular girl. I really want to drop a bomb on her and tell her that her boyfriend in high school was cheating on her. There she is!

"Oh my god, hi Tanya, how are you? You look fantastic!"

I am a complete chicken liver and cannot say anything mean to you right now, goddamn it, but hey you are just as cold a bitch as I remember. She barely gives me the time of day and walks off. I am so disappointed in myself.

Wow, who is this now approaching me? Oh, it's Marlene Dawson. She was always really nice, and I never gave her the time of day. What? She lives two blocks away from me now! That's incredible. Sure, I will meet her for coffee sometime. She runs a book club! I would love to join. Thanks for the number. Text me any time. Amazing!

Oh my god, there's the blond-haired god that I secretly had a ginormous crush on all through high school. I used to follow behind him on the way home just to stare at his long blond hair and faded jean jacket, and I found out where he lived when he turned off two streets before mine. I would fantasize about going to his house for a make-out sesh on Friday night. His parents would be out, and we would go down in the basement for some heavy petting. This was a masturbation mainstay for like three years. What, he is single now? How can that be? Oh, he is recently divorced. Well, too bad I'm married or I'd have to go up to him right now and tell him how much I loved him and maybe we were meant to be together after all. I suddenly feel like I'm thirteen again.

I was shocked to learn that nearly half of our teachers are dead. There are photos of them on a giant screen with famous captions of advice they gave us back in 1980. Mr. Jamieson always said, "Don't be a burnout." Mrs. Rogers, the math teacher, always said, "Save ten percent of your wages for a rainy day." Principal Macdonald said, "Show your parents what you can do." It all seemed so cheesy. Why couldn't they talk to us like real people? The only interesting one was from the drama teacher, Miss Carlisle, who always told us at the end of every class, "Everyone's life is mediocre, so if you want to stand out from the crowd, be dramatic!" She was right. I fondly remember the loud, funny pranksters from my workplace who kept the mood bright even on a rainy Monday. They were in the drama class.

Let's talk about family reunions for a moment. Here is advice from somebody who has zero relatives living anywhere on this continent: if you can make this happen, do it! I have been to my husband's family reunions twice, and they are fantastic. You will never feel that connected to a group of people anywhere else, and the old stories you will hear are important to share with your kids before they are lost forever. The photos you take will become treasured memories for them. The more alcohol you can consume together, the better the stories will be. Make it a potluck affair or get it catered so everyone can join the discussion. Play some table games or yard games to keep it light. Don't be thinking that your place is not good enough or the drive out of town is too far; make it happen! You won't regret it.

Finally, workplace reunions are fun too. My husband gets together with his old warehouse crew once a year for dinner at a local spaghetti house. They drink and laugh about old times and tell stories of who they pranked and which boss was cool, which one was a ball-breaker, and who was sleeping with Darlene in accounting. There is a whole lingo around every workplace that only a select few people in your life are privy to. They can talk about the Bendi B3 forklift and the loading docks and bays and the boiler room and canteen. It's fun to speak that language again and go back to a younger time.

I meet with my retired teacher friends once or twice a year to rehash old memories and report back on new adventures. It's a very therapeutic reunion and reminds me of everything I accomplished as a teacher for thirty years. It's easy to forget how hard you worked on a day-to-day basis once you retire. I had so many interactions with kids, and I may even have made a meaningful difference in some of their lives. I have had a few kids come back to me as young adults and thank me in various ways, either through a mutual contact or via social media. It is always rewarding to see them grown up and successful. Just the fact that they remember me is humbling.

So do try to reconnect. You can even be the one who posts the invite or makes the phone calls to make these reunions happen. It only takes one person to get the ball rolling, and it's always worth it. You might even rekindle an old friendship that turns into a nice surprise.

Chapter Fifteen

Minimizing Our Footprint

D uring this pandemic, it seems people are returning to a simpler way of life. People are becoming more self-reliant out of necessity; they don't want to go into shops for fear of exposure. Many are trying out some of the more ancient arts, such as growing and canning their own food, cooking instead of ordering takeout, repairing furniture and various other handiworks. Some are into building things like model cars, war figures or airplanes, bird feeders, doll houses or shelving. Other artists are busy making pottery bowls, painting, weaving cloth or knitting hats. These are all wonderfully worthwhile pursuits and make us joyful in our creativity. I would never discourage anyone from spending their time creating beautiful things. It's lovely to have a studio or creative space set up in your home that is your sanctuary. I love attending craft fairs and usually buy all my Christmas and birthday presents there because I believe in supporting local artisans.

However, from a parent's perspective, I currently have about forty of my daughter's paintings in my basement. Of course, I love every one of them because she is my child, but let's be real. I have been schlepping them around with me from home to home for the past fifteen years as she left for university and travelled the world. She still hasn't really laid down roots anywhere at nearly thirty, so I am stuck with them for the time being. There are way too many to hang on my walls.

So, I would encourage all you creatives to either use, sell or give away your wares as much as possible. We think our children will want all these collections when we die, but they really don't. They might want one particular piece, and we can give it to them now instead of waiting. The rest we should enjoy sharing with friends as gifts or with strangers by selling them at craft fairs, pawn shops or online. We should try to travel light at this stage of our lives. Our children will appreciate having as little to deal with as possible when we leave this Earth. Once you have gone through this process with your own parents, you will realize this is the truth. I did not want my father's collection of *Architectural Digest* magazines or my mother's collection of baskets. Nor does my stepson want my husband's collection of baseball cards. We have to be realistic and deal with whittling down our own belongings.

While we're on the subject of giving stuff away, let's talk about money. Some people have a little, some people have a lot, some people have none. Some of us leave this planet with a pile of credit card debt that their kids have to somehow address, which is unfortunate.

Recently, I have known numerous friends who have lost their parents and received no inheritance at all because everything was left to a second or third spouse who had only been in the picture for a very short period of time. I always shake my head when I hear this. Why would anyone leave all their money to a spouse they've known for two or three years and not provide for their kids? It's baffling and so hurtful. My friends who've been on the receiving end of this are shattered by it. They feel unseen and unloved by their parents, even in their fifties and sixties. Even if they left a small amount or a valuable or meaningful heirloom, it would be better than nothing at all. To be ignored in favour of the latest romantic entanglement is harsh. I strongly urge everyone to put their children first, even if there has been bad blood in the past, in fact, even more so then. The gesture will mend damaged relationships and leave the kids with a more loving feeling about you.

Now is the time to share your wealth, if you have any, with the people who are important to you. Take your children and grandchildren out for supper or on a family vacation. Buy your grandkids a favourite toy or a new outfit or some art supplies or books for college. It can be something as small as a trip to the dollar store with the younger ones. If you don't have money, give them the gift of your time. Get down on the floor and play with them when they're little. Offer to babysit if you're physically able to. Cook a meal and bring it over to them when they are tired from working all day. If you don't live in the same town you can mail them a grocery store gift card or ask them to FaceTime with you on Sundays. Try and be an active participant in their lives to show you care. They will remember these acts of kindness for the rest of their lives and think of you as part of their support team.

We have time now to think about our environmental footprint on this planet and how we can keep it as small as possible. The next two generations of family will respect us for considering this. Hoarding has no place in this equation. They will support your decision to downsize your home, to recycle judiciously, to trade in your gas-guzzling vehicle for a small electric one, to grow your own vegetables. They can even help you with this if you are physically unable to do so. You can ask your grandkids or hire a local teenager to set up a planter box for you or to collect your larger recyclables and take them to the local waste management centre. Let's try and be part of the solution. Even though we're older, it's never too late.

There are several environmental stewardship clubs in every town. These conservation groups are another great way to meet people and give something back. I am interested in the local salmon enhancement stream protection society. I could see myself pulling weeds along the riverbank or volunteering at the tiny hatchery down the road. Anything that saves the Earth and engages the mind and body is worthwhile. You can adopt a street and pick up trash with a set of long-handled tongs while you're out on your daily walk. You can take a plot at the community garden or keep bee-friendly tubes, bird boxes or feeders in your yard. Perhaps you might enjoy being a docent for children's field trips to a park or nature facility. If you want your grandchildren to admire you and engage in conversation more, this is a great place to start.

There are so many options for joining in activities that we really have no excuse for feeling bored in our retirement. Choose something that is meaningful to you. Even if it's just once a week you will feel happier and more engaged to be a part of something outside your home. If you are stuck indoors due to a physical disability then you can invite people over by setting up a Meetup Group online for people who share a particular interest and ask a friend or support worker to come to the first session for safety. Something like a book club or crafting group works well indoors regardless of mobility issues. If you prefer a virtual meeting, you can use platforms like Zoom or Microsoft Teams. Ask your local librarian, any younger tech-savvy relative or a friend's child to help you.

My own writing group meets weekly to share their work at a coffee shop. Sometimes we go for lunch afterwards, and I have made new friends there. Book clubs are great for this too. There is a local walking group I'm thinking of joining that meet at a local park two mornings a week. I only have time for one morning, but they won't care. You can always find somebody who matches your pace to chat with. I also recently joined a watercolour painting class that has an equal number of men and women, and it was thoroughly enjoyable. There are even wine and art nights in many community centres now where you get to drink and make art at the same time. So much fun! You can learn woodwork, jewelry making, pottery, carving or any other craft that interests you.

There's even a local singles club for over fifties that holds regular socials at the legion and pub nights around town. So, if you're single, this is your chance to get out there and meet people. There are plenty of people who have lost their spouse and are looking for companionship just like you. It's especially nice to invite out friends who have lost their spouse recently to remind them that they are still important.

As seniors, we can now audit a university class at a lower cost than the young adult student body. Have you always been interested in archeology or Russian history or wanted to learn another language? Now is the time to explore all these interests that have been percolating in your mind for years. If there's no university near you then try a local community college or adult education centre. They even have computer classes for pure beginners who missed the boat on technology. This time around it will be for pleasure, with no pressure to get good grades.

Try to get out and enjoy community events. You now have the time to attend concerts, plays, galleries, trade shows and farmer's markets like never before. Keep an eye on your local events page either online or in the newspaper. There are even retirement fairs at the convention centre annually in most major cities with loads of sponsors who wish to tap into our every desire. You can buy every health gadget there, from a foot massager to a vibrator, and they will connect you to nationwide service networks for seniors that you've never even heard of. If you're not comfortable driving or riding transit, then take a Lyft or an Uber. There's a whole world out there to explore.

Chapter Sixteen

Death Planning

We touched on this issue of inheritance in the last chapter, but let's dive a little deeper into the issue of end-of-life planning. I know this topic scares a lot of people, but it's really important. I recently knew a couple my age who believed that if they made a will, they would immediately die in some freak accident. We finally convinced them how important it was, especially since they had a dependent physically disabled adult daughter who required a care plan. Now is the time to get it together, put your irrational fears aside and make a will.

There are plenty of online resources to help you do this on the cheap. You can draft one yourself using the forms provided on the web and then take it to a notary for filing if you want to save money. Otherwise, you can have a notary or lawyer guide you through the process for around $1000 (as of 2020). Either way, wills can be very simple or very detailed.

Simple is better. For example, you will leave your assets to be divided among your children equally, and you choose two reliable people you trust with your bank accounts as executors (they must agree to this). If you don't have children, then you can leave your assets to a sibling, a friend, a charity, anyone you wish. If you do not have a will, everything you own will sit in probate for a long time and there is a lot more hassle dealing with everything, from paying your final rent to getting back a damage deposit. You need to appoint an executor to act on your behalf or none of this will happen.

You also need to make two other documents. The first is called Power of Attorney (POA), and the second is a Representation Agreement (RA). These are in the event that you have a terrible car accident and somebody has to take care of your decisions for a while. Power of Attorney lets another person do your banking and financial decision-making while you're sick or injured, or later on if you're in a care home. The Rep Agreement allows someone (can be the same person) to make medical decisions for you, such as grant permission to do surgery, keep you on life support or pull the plug. Needless to say, this should be someone you love and trust more than anyone and whom you share your final wishes with ahead of time. Would you rather receive a lethal dose of morphine than be left in a coma or in pain for years on end? Do you want your ashes scattered in a particular place? You need to spell this out to them, and you can include this in a living will section as well. These people should ideally live in the same town as you because you will never know ahead of time when they will be called upon, hopefully never.

I am grateful that my mother communicated all this and helped me make all her arrangements beforehand. I used the Power of Attorney document frequently when caring for my mother in the final ten years of her life when she was unable to drive or walk much. I did all her shopping and banking, and the best thing she ever did was to create a joint bank account with me while she was still able-bodied. I was able to send a copy of the POA document to all her work and various pensions, deal with her doctors, get her medications and file her taxes. Veteran's Affairs helped pay for her wheelchair and electric lift armchair, which would have been very expensive otherwise. She also put me on joint title on her house, which meant that the house didn't have to sit in government probate after she died before I could sell it.

Her will was clear, simple and named me as executrix. She had also gradually divvied up her treasured belongings between my sister and I over the last ten years of her life, so everything was done. I was extremely lucky to have such a caring, responsible parent, and I know how rare this is. Conversely, when my sister died, her house sat in probate for a year and a half before I could sell it and give her sons their inheritance. I have heard other people say they can't even broach the topic of estate planning with their aged parents because it's too awkward. I truly feel for them. It's critical to talk to your children/executors ahead of time and take these steps to make their lives easier after you're gone. Your loved ones will truly appreciate your efforts to set these plans up when you get older, need care and eventually pass on.

Now let's talk about the emotional aspect of dying. There are almost as many schools of thought on the subject as there are people on Earth. You may be a member of one of the big three faiths: Christianity, Islam or Judaism, or any of the multitude of other religions. You may be an atheist or agnostic or you may follow the tenets of a more New-Age thinker, such as Eckhart Tolle or Deepak Chopra. Whatever your beliefs are, you may never really know how you feel until faced with old age if you are lucky enough, or a long-term illness or an urgent health crisis. When your cards are all laid out on the table, so to speak, then your faith and/or fears will be brought to the forefront. I truly hope that when the time comes, you will find solace in whatever belief system you have chosen.

I was raised by two atheists. My father lost all faith after losing his parents in the Holocaust. My mother attended the Anglican Church as a child but became a believer of pure science as an adult. She always said to just throw her on the compost heap when she died. She said she believed that death was a black void of nothingness and scoffed at every esoteric idea, such as psychic abilities, tarot, even horoscopes, as being utter poppycock. I was never taken to any church, except with a friend occasionally to play music for her mother's choir.

However, lo and behold, at age ninety-something and in a care home, the only books she wanted to keep from the house were her beloved murder mysteries and a Bible. She said she valued it only as a literary work for the stories, but I have my doubts. From watching this, I learned that fear creeps in for all of us in the end and we grasp at any comfort we can find. Those childhood lessons run deep, and I wonder how I will fare with my inexperience. Do I need to find faith before it's too late?

I am open to some of the newer schools of thought because my daughter has exposed me to a lot of them. She started seeing spirits and reporting it to me from a very young age. How do you not believe your own child when she repeatedly and innocently describes in detail the ghosts that visit her bedroom every night? How does a four-year-old make these things up when she has never been exposed to anything remotely similar? She really got me thinking about alternate realities, I can tell you that.

During her late teens and early twenties, she was channelling other people's dead loved ones and had some amazing experiences, which are only hers to tell. She did tell me that my father was still in our house after he died and was watching over my aged mother; somehow this was comforting to me. As an adult, she has reported much fewer encounters with spirit, but she does meditate every day and has a lot of strange, inexplicable encounters with animals. Owls seem to follow her around frequently, and one morning she opened the front door and a hawk was sitting on the stoop staring at her. I don't know what to make of it, but I'm open to the possibilities.

Recently I've been listening to videos by some of the New Age spiritual gurus, such as Eckhart Tolle, Deepak Chopra and Ram Dass. They have opened my mind to alternative ways of seeing our existence here on Earth and the universal fear of dying. Ram Dass talks about how our society treats dying as a failure of the medical system and there's all this fear and hysterical denial about what is happening. He said that if we just observe and accept death as a natural part of the journey back into our thousands of reincarnations, it becomes like a new beginning. He advised people to use dying as a vehicle of awakening.[1]

Deepak Chopra talks about how the real you is an eternal timeless being that is continually reincarnated. "Those cells [in your body] are being born and they're dying all at the moment, all the time, eternally and timeless now."[2] His ideas make me think that I am just a speck of sentient dust, a part of something so much bigger than myself.

Eckhart Tolle shares a similar idea when he talks about "the one consciousness." He says, "I am just a consciousness enclosed in matter, like inside my body. My energy field or consciousness or essence of being never dies, it just goes back to the source."[2]

Someday I may be able to define what my own beliefs are, but right now they are a hodgepodge of disconnected ideas without clarity. Buddhism seems like

[1] Ram Dass, "Perspectives on Death-Pt.1 Sept.30, 2014 viewed onYouTube. 2 Chopra, Deepak. "If I am Eternal, then why do I disappear upon death?" Feb. 5, 2020 viewed on YouTube

[2] Eckhart Tolle, "What Happens When We Die?" Oct. 15, 2015, viewed on YouTube.

a nice religion and I like the Baha'i ideal of one world government, but other than that I am just floating along out here. I am definitely not inspired by Christianity; to me the Bible is just a book written two thousand years ago about a man who others admired. There has been so much ill will towards so many minority groups in the name of god that I cannot buy into big religion. There is so much hate mongering between the big three (Christianity, Islam and Judaism) that none of them seem loving and inclusive. I would like to learn more about the many Asian religions. Perhaps they have more peaceful kindness to offer.

I believe in the pure sciences and the powers of modern pharmaceuticals, and I will obediently take whatever my doctor prescribes. In contrast, I enjoy a nice tarot card or psychic reading because it is fun, and I can take it with a grain of salt. I guess I'm a sympathetic sceptic. I am not subscribing whole heartedly to any of these philosophies, but I am curious to explore different world views on dying so that, when the time does come, I might be less afraid. If these new age ideas sound crazy to you, then perhaps you can show me the way.

Chapter Seventeen

Love in a Time of COVID

I realize that in sharing my personal story, I have neglected all my readers who cannot possibly relate to being in a happy marriage at this point in their lives. I know many people are suffering from loneliness, and some of my closest girlfriends have given up hope and resigned themselves to being alone for the rest of their lives, which makes me sad. Some have endured bad experiences that left them jaded, and others simply lack the self-confidence to put themselves out there. I notice people my age and a little older who are walking their dogs or shopping with a particular far-away look in their eyes that tells me their spouse has died and they are grieving. I dread this day myself, as it must be the hardest thing ever to deal with, second only to the loss of a child.

I have also noticed a huge increase in mental health issues during this pandemic. When I chat with people on Twitter, many openly express their struggles with anxiety, depression, bipolar disorder and even schizophrenia. Then there is a whole group of LGBTQI folks who are expressing themselves for the first time in history about their own struggles with identity, acceptance and relationships. It is wonderful that the current generation is able to speak openly about their medical issues without fear of reprisal, but what concerns me are the sheer numbers at this time who need support. My American friends are telling me they don't have access to adequate treatment because they can't afford medical insurance, especially if they are out of work due to COVID-19. It is a nasty cycle. Here in Canada, at least we can talk to our doctor online and get a prescription renewed or a referral to a therapist, psychiatrist or specialist doctor.

In the United States right now, people are afraid to even leave their homes because the daily number of new cases is so high and there are still protesters gathering in the streets every night in major cities as part of the Black Lives Matter movement. It is an important message, to be sure, but the timing is unfortunate because these protesters are putting themselves at risk of exposure to the virus by gathering in large groups. Then there are other groups of right-wing extremists gathering to protest wearing masks, saying it is undue government control, which is ridiculous. All this upheaval is affecting people's moods almost as much as COVID-19. Some small business owners are not only struggling to make ends meet, they are also having their windows smashed and their merchandise stolen by looters in some cities. Curfews have been imposed and the National Guard has been called in to try and keep order, but this is viewed as further police brutality. It is a terrible time to be alone with your thoughts, never mind trying to meet someone new for friendship or romance. It seems that everyone's life is on hold for the foreseeable future.

The fear of getting out there again is compounded for some older people by a lack of technical knowledge in how to use a computer. Some of my generation have worked in fields where they never developed computing skills, like my husband who was a transit driver. He has only basic computer knowledge and needs a lot of support with online tasks. The idea of creating an online dating profile with a photo and a write-up is terrifying, never mind checking an app and connecting with strangers. Factor in any shyness and I can understand why many people never get a foot out the door. I can only encourage you to ask for help if you find yourself in this situation. There are basic computing skills classes for seniors at most local libraries or continuing education through the school district's evening and summer classes. This will open up a whole world of social media to connect you to friends, relatives and potential partners. Think of how care-home patients' faces light up when they FaceTime with their loved ones. It is no coincidence that most people are spending hours on their phone each day connecting on Instagram, Twitter and other sites; it is fun to engage with others! But to combat loneliness, you must be willing to take those first steps to learn something new.

We are never too old for online connections. There are a multitude of websites offering their services for a fee of between $10-$40 per month (in 2020), such as:

Senior Match, eHarmony, Elite Singles, Silver Singles, Sixty and Me, Senior Friend Finder, Our Time and Zoosk. They will guide you through the process and find local people for you to have coffee with, if nothing more. You are always in the driver's seat and can accept or refuse suggestions. If I were single at this point in my life, I would definitely join one of these services. Being alone sucks! Even if you don't meet a sexual partner, you may just meet the greatest new friend or roommate to share your life with.

If you find the idea of starting a new sexual relationship really scary or gross at this time in your life, I've got news for you. Seniors have some of the most amazing sex of their lives because there is no more time for bullshit or head games about performance, appearance, jealousy or attachment. At this stage of our lives, most people can say what they want and just get on with it. Romance is still an option for sure, but if you're more of a no-frills person you can make that clear from the start. If you're not looking to move in with someone ever again, you can tell them right out of the gate in your profile blurb. If you've had a mastectomy or colon cancer has led to erectile dysfunction and you need to take Viagra, all this is open for discussion. There is no time for pussyfooting around these issues. We all have baggage at this age; it's unavoidable. Embrace your life and get on with it!

We all have physical flaws up the wazoo as well. Nobody over fifty looks good naked unless they are a rare specimen like Christie Brinkley or have paid for multiple surgeries, which will leave severe scarring anyhow. We all have sagging breasts and balls. We all have wrinkles and moles and skin tags. We all have aches and pains and difficulty getting into any bathing suit or Kama Sutra position, so just admit it, laugh at yourselves and enjoy every moment of your short, ordinary life! Stop thinking you are so different or more special than anyone else. I assure you that the next person's problems are as real as yours, but they just need to be explained before you go into the bedroom.

Once you get there, it will all have been worth it. Even if you only end up kissing and cuddling, that is lovely and way better than spending another night alone. If you finish up in wild orgasms, that's just a bonus. You may have just found the greatest lover of your life so enjoy it, even if they don't have any money or share your world view. Sex is wonderful for your mental and physical health, so meet this person again. You can even tell them it's only for the sex; they might just be flattered and feel the same way about you.

I would also encourage you to consider your list of friends for anyone who you are compatible enough to live with, especially if they have lost their partner recently. You can maintain your own privacy within a shared space by moving into a separate suite or an upstairs-downstairs or shared kitchen arrangement. You can just meet in the common areas for part of the day to cook, talk or watch TV. Having another person to share responsibilities like taking out the trash, gardening, snow-clearing, running errands or grocery shopping can be a godsend. Just knowing there's another caring person there when you are sick will put your mind at ease and be mutually beneficial. Many of us do not have children or relatives living nearby so this is smart for companionship and safety.

Please don't give up hope if you are alone. It only takes one first step to ask for help and you will be on your way to meeting a new friend, which is all anybody needs to lift their spirits. If you are shy, then drop into the seniors' centre and ask to see a counsellor there. They can connect you to all manner of services and groups that might fit your interests. Just getting out of the house for any type of interaction with others might allow you to meet someone special, even if it turns into a completely platonic connection.

I know several retired seniors who were alone, have been lucky enough to meet a lovely partner and remarry and are now travelling the world on their second honeymoon. We are all lonely and vulnerable to varying degrees, so don't be afraid. There is definitely someone out there for you, even if it's only for long-term friendship and company.

Chapter Eighteen

The Many Vices of Eve

ave you ever walked into a bar at noon, perhaps
on the way to a beach or brunch party to buy
off-sales, and seen that one table of sad old
men who are there every day sucking on their first beer
of what will be a long series? Their spouse may have
died, or if she's still alive she has long since accepted that
this is his routine and he won't be home until supper
time, when he'll eat whatever plate she plops in front of
him and pass out in his chair in front of the TV. This is
the land of the living dead, and you do not want to be
a part of it.

Addiction to booze and gambling runs rampant
in my husband's family. He comes from a long line of
card sharks and bet placers, and many of them are now
into poker, slot machines, lottery and Keno tickets. My
husband is very drawn to all of it, especially playing
poker and craps, but he keeps it under control. We love
going to the casino and the horse races a couple of times
a year. We play extremely small stakes poker games at

home with friends. Thank god he completely shuns any online betting as the root of all evil.

Alcoholism has touched his life very closely on all sides of his family, including both parents, who found sobriety later in life. His father swore by Alcoholics Anonymous and attended meetings religiously. His mother quit cold turkey and never looked back. His stepfather famously left his bladder cancer recovery bed in hospital, grabbed a walker and marched down the hospital sidewalk in his dressing gown to buy a box of wine. Never has a man been more motivated to do anything.

My husband and I have about fifteen close friends and relatives who are alcoholics. Most of them are men. He has lost friends over booze—the ones who called him a judgmental prick via email at three a.m. because of their own shame. He has been called the boring guy at the party so many times when everyone around him is pissed out of their tree, but then they still shamelessly ask him for a ride home. He has hugged giant sobbing men as they admitted their pain and failure to him in the wee hours of their despair. He has watched beloved cousins go bankrupt just as their kids grew into an age when they could understand what was happening. Through it all, he has remained cheerful and supportive and kept himself to two glasses of wine or two beers a night.

Some research says that marijuana cannot be addictive, but I've seen differently. They say it's just the behavioural component of getting high that is the addiction; maybe so. Splitting hairs in my opinion. I once dated a guy who would become super grouchy when he was jonesing for a puff. We once had to drive back from an outing just so he could maintain his usual level of reefer madness. It looked like an addiction to me.

And then there's porn. I have heard only two men in my life admit that they were addicted to porn, but if I know two who are "out" about it, then everyone must know somebody who is keeping it hidden. It seems to be more of a male habit, but that is no doubt a sexist remark. I'm sure there are women, too, even soccer moms, who really are into watching porn. We once caught our teenage son watching it with a friend and had to inform the other kid's parents. That was not fun. Sex is available everywhere your phone goes, and if you're retired and have a lot of free time, this proclivity can be exacerbated. There is help available, just like for any other addiction.

Women seem to prefer pills. My sister always loved Ativan and Percocet, and then she also got addicted to pain pills during her cancer treatment. In her last year she was seen taking fourteen Tylenol 2s at once. The nurse said if she kept it up, it would kill her. After she died, as her executrix, I was shocked to read in her medical reports that she was also labelled an alcoholic. I never saw her drink to excess. Maybe that clinician was wrong? I will never know. I do know that she was addicted to smoking pot and cigarettes her entire life, starting both at age thirteen. She must have had the constitution of a horse to be able to tolerate all these substances in her system for so long.

Growing up, my best friend's mom was the stereotypically perfect seventies Avon-Lady-middle-aged housewife. She wore hot pink pant suits and sold everything from vacuums to condos. I realized later that she was addicted to nasal spray and ended up having an operation on her nose that was never really talked about openly. Many women were dependent on Valium in the sixties and seventies because doctors regularly supplied it to alleviate everything from headaches to "bad nerves," which was the description given for the general malaise of the impermeable glass ceiling at that time. Two doors down from us was my other friend's mom who drank rye and ginger from morning to night. I spent summers at their cabin, and my parents never realized a drunk woman was around driving me all day. She was the kindest person ever, and her husband was an abusive drunk asshole. It's amazing how well their three daughters turned out, considering.

Shopping addiction is also a real phenomenon. I have known three people who suffered from this, especially online shopping. This can be extremely destructive to a relationship, just like any other addiction. These people can spend a month's rent or mortgage payment in one afternoon to fill some kind of emotional void in their lives. Receiving packages in the mail full of new clothes or gadgets is apparently the same kind of high as you get from drugs. Seeking treatment is important, otherwise bankruptcy and shame are the inevitable outcomes.

And then there's TV. So many seniors spend their days in front of the boob tube. I refuse to turn it on before six in the evening as some measure of control.

I have never understood the draw of daytime soaps or talk shows. I'm sorry if this sounds judgmental, but I see this as a complete waste of time. If this is your thing, I would encourage you to go outside or read a book instead. You are missing out on real life! When my husband was a teenager, he used to race home at lunch, make ramen noodles, sit in front of the TV, and then call his mother at work on her lunch break to give her the play by play on *All My Children*. I am not making this up. This was before VCRs could record a show. Yes, he is a mama's boy, but he would usually skip school for the rest of the day to get high and hang out with his cousin, so, win-win.

Why am I telling you this? Because now that we have retired and have a lot of free time on our hands, any vices that have been lying just under the surface will probably try to rear their ugly heads. I worry about the number of prescription drugs I'm taking, especially pain pills. So far I have "maintained" on daily Ibuprofen, but my back pain is getting steadily worse. I have three herniated disks, and I know that codeine, Vicodin or OxyContin could be around the corner, but I'm lucky enough to have a fantastic doctor who is referring me for cortisone injections before that happens. Prescription drug addiction is a huge problem among seniors, and I intend to avoid it for as long as possible. I have known a few young people who have died from overdoses of Fentanyl thinking they were taking something more benign. It has become a crisis in Vancouver and many other parts of North America.

If you have a tendency to enjoy drinking or drugs just a little too much, now is the time to be honest with your doctor because we are drawn to these even more with too much time on our hands. This is no way to live. I implore you to seek help if you have these tendencies. Talk to your doctor as you head into retirement. Be very honest; they have seen it all. There is treatment available even if you don't have money. You are heading into what should be the best part of your life. You don't want to ruin it by numbing all the goodness out of it and impoverishing yourself in the process. You don't want to become the family embarrassment who is remembered with a chuckle and then quickly forgotten as a joke. Addiction is an illness, and nobody is immune. My girlfriend who went into rehab after she retired says it was the best thing she ever did. She says she feels happier than ever before because her senses are no longer numbed by booze every day. Her family is so thrilled to have her back as a fully-functioning mother and grandmother.

If you have lived too long with a partner who is addicted, then you also need support. Go to Al-anon or Nar-anon meetings or individual therapy to get that lifelong accumulation of toxic feelings out of your body and mind once and for all. You don't deserve to spend your golden years as a victim of abuse or neglect. Seeing a professional can help you decide whether you want to put in the effort to salvage the relationship or get the hell out.

It is hard work to overcome any addiction, but once you realize you have a problem and decide to seek help, you have already faced the most challenging aspect. Now is the time to embrace the best part of your life and enjoy every day to its fullest. This may sound cheesy, but you only get one time around the bases and that time is now.

Chapter Nineteen

Create Your Own Bucket List

N ow that you have arrived at retirement or are approaching sixty, whichever comes first, you should be making your own bucket list. By this I mean actually writing it down, keeping it in a place that's visible to you every day and starting to plan how you're going to achieve and cross off one item at a time. Now is the time to make your dreams come true. Realistically, by seventy-five most of us will have some serious physical health restrictions so we have fifteen more good years to get 'er done.

If you don't have much money, there are lots of ways to travel on the cheap. There are home exchange organizations, and you don't need to live in a mansion because a small apartment will do fine. There are loads of international volunteer organizations, such as charities and churches, who will take you abroad in exchange for teaching English to the locals for a few hours a week, or to teach any other useful life skills you may know. There are beaches in the world where you can live comfortably for $10 a day, for example in Southeast Asia. If you stay off the beaten track and ask the locals where the deals are, you will save a bundle. You are now free to travel during the lowest of low seasons and shop for the best possible airfares.

A few couples I know have opted for the RV lifestyle. One of these couples even sold their home to accomplish this dream of living on the road around North America with no attachments. They just rented a postal box in a fixed address to keep receiving their mail and gave a trusted friend the key to empty it and message them if there was anything important. This way they could keep residency status and keep receiving their pensions via direct deposit while they were gone. They are loving life with no certain destination and no time restraints. They post some of the best photos, and their lives look fantastic. They are very social and meet new people wherever they go. The only drawback seems to be the high cost of medical insurance.

You should think about personal safety at this point in your life. Travelling in pairs is ideal, but there are also small group travel organizations for like-minded seniors and women available, such as designated tours for art, history, cooking or archeology enthusiasts. Check your local seniors' publications, the back personal ads section of newspapers or conduct online searches. Talk to your doctor if you have any health issues, and always get good travel health insurance. Take extra medications with you and over-the-counter remedies for tummy trouble and minor ailments, which may not be available where you're going. Get whatever shots you need at a travel clinic, and keep your domestic shots, like tetanus, up to date.

Tell people where you are going if you like to travel off the beaten path. Even if I'm just going for a hike near home, I always text my route and my expected return time to somebody, and I carry water, bear spray and a snack in case I get lost. This goes double when you're abroad in unknown parts. Ask the locals which areas are safe, which creatures are harmful, and make sure there is cellular reception. We are not as tough as we used to be, so we need to rely on our smarts.

The other non-travel items on your bucket list are probably closer to home. Perhaps you have always wanted to ride a horse or you never learned to learn how to swim. Don't let embarrassment hold you back. Take those tango or music lessons or buy yourself that kayak. You can't take it with you, so splurge on yourself right now!

We live near a river so I wanted to take up kayaking, but my husband said if he ever got into a kayak I'd have to call the fire department to bring the Jaws of Life to extricate his ass from it because he has an old hip injury from working in a warehouse. So I am on my own. For me, it's my bladder that holds me back from doing lengthy outdoor activities. I always have to check if there's a washroom available nearby. Those ads on the TV for grown lady pull-ups are no longer amusing to me. I'm not there yet, but I don't need a crystal ball to see where this is headed. However, I am determined not to let it slow me down.

I decided to ask a friend named Deborah, who owns two kayaks, to help me try it out first. She picked me up and took me to a little sandy spit along the dykes. We changed into aqua shoes and unloaded her roof rack, carrying them individually across the parking area and down to the water. Getting in was interesting and required some careful positioning in the shallows and some balanced footing. Once I got going, it was very gentle movement and serene. We saw a couple of sleek, furry black minks slithering along the banks. They were so skinny I thought they were water snakes at first. Then we saw a bear eating blackberries, and I panicked. Deborah quietly directed me, and we carefully paddled towards the opposite bank of the river to just float by without incident.

After forty minutes we turned around and began paddling against the current. This was harder work, and I started to feel the burn in my arms and shoulders. I knew I'd be sore the next day. When we got back, Deborah steadied the kayak to let me climb out, and I realized this would be tricky on my own. I ran for the port-a-potty in the parking lot, desperate for a pee. Afterwards, I had a little difficulty lifting the kayak myself. I realized that Chris would have to help me load/unload it, which is something to consider if you live alone. I just needed to get a roof rack on my car, but I was feeling inspired. I learned that it's best to try something new before making a decision to spend a chunk of money on a new toy.

Many people with physical limitations are purchasing electric bicycles now as a great way to get exercise and explore their own neighbourhoods without strenuous effort. Look around at what others are doing and see what excites you. Get your heart level elevated about something new and quit making excuses why you can't do it. A little positive thinking goes a long way towards getting off the couch.

I know what you're thinking. She is sitting there at home on her high horse writing away about doing exciting things and she hasn't even got dressed for the past two days. You would be right! However, for me, having the time to write has been my lifelong dream. I know that some of you will feel very happy and fulfilled just reading a good book, playing the piano or having coffee with a friend, and that's wonderful. But I have found that whenever I try just one new thing, it gives me a tremendous sense of accomplishment.

For example, I recently took just three golf lessons and started going to the driving range, and now I am playing par three courses with my husband and really enjoying myself. It made me feel young again to be a pure beginner listening to an instructor. It's healthy to admit you know nothing about a subject and start from scratch, and you will probably be cultivating new areas of your brain that were previously untapped. Bonus: learning a new task is helpful in fending off Alzheimer's disease.

My husband's dreams are closer to home. He wants a viper red 1967 Camaro, like the group of older men I see meeting at the diner by my gym every Saturday morning in their old classic cars to have breakfast and swap carburetor stories. The only problem is my husband has no mechanical aptitude whatsoever (sorry, Darling) but he loves the idea of driving around feeling like a teenager again. He is waiting for me to relent and say this is a great way to spend our savings, which is not likely to happen anytime soon. I am such a mean wife.

What I'm saying is that you don't need to travel to a remote part of the world to cross something off your bucket list. I'm sure this particular group of men (and women) probably feel great joy when polishing their chrome trim and driving around getting jealous looks from seventeen-year-old boys and girls. Do whatever makes you happy. I just can't relate, even though I used to ride and polish a motorcycle for ten years. Yes, I'm clearly a hypocrite.

My mother used to get excited over receiving a new stamp in the mail for her collection. My husband collects coins and baseball cards. Whenever he looks at them, he remembers a whole story about where and when he bought that card, the conversation and haggling with the owner, and all the teams he watched that athlete play for and their stats. He has an incredible mind for these details, just don't ask him where his keys are.

I recommended in an earlier chapter to get rid of these collections before you die because your kids won't want them. But if they still bring you joy, then by all means pursue collecting. There will be like-minded people in your local area to meet up and chat with about whatever trinkets you enjoy. My friend makes jewelry and handbags to sell at craft fairs. There is a local crafters guild for that, too, as well as a local lapidary club where she can learn about and buy crystals. If there isn't a group in your town then you can easily initiate one by placing an ad online using Meetup or some other platform.

So, get out there and enjoy life while you still can. There are so many wonderful things to do now that you're not working. Don't be afraid. We are all just as inexperienced and awkward as you are. Just put on a comfortable pair of shoes and get on with it because, as my mother-in-law always says, the years seem to pass by faster than the days.

Chapter Twenty

The Ultimate Cat

A t the age of sixty, if you are a responsible pet owner, you suddenly realize that when your beloved pet dies, the next one you adopt from the animal shelter will be the last cat of your life, since they can easily live for twenty years. This is a strange realization because you begin to take stock of all the cats who have delineated your life with their reassuring presence. Chris' mother had fourteen at one point, my parents only had five at the apex of our family togetherness. I remember them all lying on the back deck or flaked out in the sun in the raised garden beds of catnip plants along the driveway in summer. They brought us great comfort and joy over the years. The ultimate cat signals your mortality in a most convincing way and gives one great pause (not paws…groan).

The last trip to the shelter is a daunting decision. Should it be a timid, ordinary brown female tabby who worships the ground you walk on and follows your lap to every location in the house? Or should it be a big bruiser tom who couldn't care less what you do as long as there's food at regular intervals? We settled on a noisy, long, skinny ginger named Buddy who spent ten minutes telling Chris his life story. We gently pushed him into the carrier and off we went.

Buddy became the most delightful occupation for the next couple of months, and we couldn't get enough of helping him adjust to his new home. Chris kept saying Buddy won the lottery because he is spared no treat or toy or cuddle. He even gets tuna once a week and regular table scraps. We fully understand how Buddy has replaced our children in every way. If this is unhealthy, we don't care.

We talk to him in ridiculously high voices and use all kinds of sickening baby-talk words like "num-nums" and "cuddles" and "fussy-wussy" and "scritches." Anyone visiting would write us off as complete lunatics. We give him way too much leeway to come under the quilt on our bed and walk on the dining table to receive scraps of our dinner that are pre-chewed for him. Gross, you say? He also gets saucers of milk and enough attention that he should be reading by now, but he is slightly delayed. These types of jokes make us way too happy.

We are both extremely grateful for our lives thus far. We have been tremendously lucky. We both had good jobs with pensions, we both had loving families and grew up in good homes, we have two healthy kids and a nice place to live. We could have been born into one of the many places of war, poverty, misery and hard-scrabble existence that are a reality in our troubled world. Fate has dealt us good cards, and we never take this for granted, especially when we see so many friends struggling financially just to get by. We will continue to donate to charities that support impoverished refugees or local food banks and homeless shelters; so many people who have nothing. Turning sixty is no joke, but we have both been so fortunate. We truly feel that any time we have left is a bonus at this point.

Chris and I recognize we could easily be happy buying a more remote property with a bit of land and an outbuilding we could convert into a cat shelter and then devoting the rest of our lives to feline care. Our friends would either think this was adorable or absolutely raving mad, but we wouldn't care. Unfortunately, we are overly practical and would be concerned about burdening our kids with inheriting a hundred stray cats, so we probably won't go this route.

The other option that is tempting for me is to set up some kind of communal living situation with a group of friends. I have been reading posts about these fantastic seniors' villages in the Netherlands and Scandinavia (which is always ahead of the curve), and the whole arrangement seems ideal. We could carefully choose some like-minded friends to invest in a large property with a few separate living spaces and share the bills, the cooking, gardening and generally looking after the place. We could call it "On Golden Age Pond." This set-up would ensure that when somebody's spouse eventually dies, they would not be isolated. Loneliness seems like the scourge of old age, and this would help eliminate it. Every time somebody died or left the group, we would invite in a new member. There would always be friends to do activities with and a shared purpose. Label me a communist if you like, but it seems like a really good option.

So, in the meantime, I chose to be a writer. I never started in earnest until I retired and had free time. As a teacher, I never had free time. I was always either prepping, working or marking, but I always felt like I should be a writer in every fibre of my being. Now I am trying to make the most of it by sharing these thoughts before it's too late. Perhaps it is my writing that will save me from feeling as though my final years were wasted watching television. It gives me purpose every morning to vent my thoughts into the ether of these pages, which will most likely never be seen. It is a catharsis that feels good because these thoughts rattle around in my head all day long and at least I'm getting them out. It feels liberating to see them in an external form released from my mind and body. If they do help anyone else understand themselves or the world around them, it is just a bonus. I am content when I'm writing, so that has value in itself.

As I cuddle Buddy, who sleeps peacefully on my lap, I think, *Yes, this will be the ultimate cat, but he will be the luckiest cat on Earth, and my mutual coexistence with this warm, loving creature is deeply gratifying.* What could be nicer than free unsolicited cuddles fifteen times a day? I strongly recommend everyone adopt a pet because they give you so much love in return with no strings attached. God bless dog people. I don't understand them, but I can appreciate them from a distance. All that lollygagging around and picking up shit doesn't sit well with me, but they seem very happy with their dog parks and truck boxes and balls and sticks.

For me, a sleeping cat is the closest thing to a real live Buddha that I can reach in this life, since I have neither the physical ability nor inclination to meditate in the forest for ten hours a day. So, live long and prosper, and may the force be with you. Let's enjoy this brief sojourn on Earth as the tiny specks of dust that we are, floating around in the universe. Namaste to all.

Bibliography

1. Ram Dass. "Perspectives on Death-Pt.1." Sept. 30, 2014. Bassett Medical Center, Cooperstown, New York, lecture, 17:52 viewed on YouTube.
2. Chopra, Deepak. "If I am Eternal, then why do I disappear upon death?" Feb. 5, 2020, Amelia Island, Florida, lecture, 26:57, viewed on YouTube.
3. Eckhart Tolle. "What Happens When We Die?" Oct. 15, 2015, New Zealand, lecture, 11:37, viewed on YouTube.

About the Author

Naomi P. Lane was born in England, but grew up in the suburbs of Vancouver Canada, where she still resides. She was a special education and French immersion teacher for thirty years and now devotes most of her time to writing. She is married to a wonderful man named Chris, and they have two adult children, who now live far away. They own one very spoiled, neurotic, tabby rescue cat named Hazel.

Her first novel, *The Ordinary Life of Nadia Lewis*, has just been published by Olympia Publishing of London. She is currently working on her third book, which will be a tale about a group of seniors living communally. When she is not writing, she enjoys reading, nature walks, travel, yoga, studying languages and following her fellow writers online. She may even visit real human beings occasionally to share coffee, tea or food, although these sightings are rare.

Please subscribe to her blog at:
www.naomiplane.com

CPSIA information can be obtained
at www.ICGtesting.com
Printed in the USA
BVHW082027230221
600842BV00001B/94

9 780228 845249